STEP INTO YOUR
BRAVE

STEP INTO YOUR BRAVE

Uplifting Stories to Inspire
Courage, Strength, and Growth

POSITIVITY LADY
PRESS

STEP INTO YOUR BRAVE

Uplifting Stories to Inspire Courage, Strength, and Growth

A LIGHTbeamers Book by April Adams Pertuis
featuring these contributing authors:
(in alphabetical order)

Beth Jones

Kristi Koehler

Dawn Loding

Kim Mittelstadt

Odeta Pine

Karen Smith

Katharina Stuerzl

Amber Wells

Copyright © 2022. Positivity Lady Press.

All rights reserved. This book or any portion thereof may not be reproduced or used in any manner whatsoever without the express written permission of the publisher except for the use of brief quotations in a book review.

Library of Congress Control Number: 2022915745
ISBN: 978-1-7327858-3-0

Positivity Lady Press
Robbinston, ME 04671
www.positivityladypress.com

This anthology is a work of creative non-fiction. All of the events depicted are true to the best of the author's memory. Some names and identifying features have been changed to protect the identity of certain parties. The author in no way represents the views of any company, corporation, or brand. Views expressed are solely those of each author.

"When you share your story, you shine a light."
— April Adams Pertuis

This book is dedicated to those who are bravely sharing their stories with the world. It matters, and you are making a significant difference.
You are a #lightbeamer.

Table of Contents

ACKNOWLEDGEMENTS xv

INTRODUCTION.. xxi

1. LISTEN TO YOUR HEART | April Adams Pertuis 1

2. GATHER YOUR COURAGE | Kristi Koehler...................... 31

3. FOCUS ON HEALING | Amber Wells............................57

4. BREAK DOWN THE WALLS | Beth Jones 73

5. REMOVE YOUR MASK | Kim Mittelstadt 101

6. BUST OUT OF THE BOX | Katharina Stuerzl 125

7. KNOW YOUR WORTH | Karen Smith........................... 155

8. RISE UP AND THRIVE | Dawn Loding........................... 179

9. CLAIM YOUR DREAMS | Odeta Pine 203

EXCERPT FROM ELEVATE YOUR VOICE:
STAND UP FOR YOURSELF | APRIL ADAMS PERTUIS............. 221

BE IN OUR NEXT BOOK 250

WORK WITH APRIL 252

ABOUT LIGHTBEAMERS... 253

ABOUT THE INSIDE STORY PODCAST................................ 255

ABOUT POSITIVITY LADY PRESS.. 256

ABOUT OUR PAY-IT-FORWARD PARTNERSHIP 258

ACKNOWLEDGEMENTS

Acknowledgements

Writing this book and others in this series takes a great many people behind the scenes — most of whom never get the credit, see their name on the back cover, or get invited to do podcast interviews during a book launch. Yet we couldn't do it without them.

A few we'd like to purposely call by name: Dyan Escolano, Christine Roxas, and Felice Perez — the amazing team members at LIGHTbeamers who pour their hearts into our projects and help us shine in countless ways. Your dedication to our mission at LIGHTbeamers is felt. Thank you for bringing your heart into everything we do, even from halfway around the world!

To our editor, Laurel Robinson. Thank you for putting so much of your time and talent into our words. Words are powerful, and you've helped us make the most of ours. Your thoughtful notes and suggestions have pushed us to be better writers, and it's been a joy to have you work on this project.

To our book designer and formatter, Ashley Hinson Dhakal. Since day one, you've been able to take our ideas and truly bring them to life on the front and back covers, and on the pages in between. Thank you!

A special thanks to fellow author and prolific writer, Emma G. Rose, for stepping in to teach our authors about the art of crafting a killer bio. Her approach really helped us take a much more fun and creative approach to writing something that can often feel extremely hard! Thank you! Thank you!!

And to our publisher and co-leader of the Lightbeamers She Gets Published Author Program, Lanette Pottle. Your guidance has been invaluable. Taking a group of women through the process of becoming first-time published authors requires a firm grip and a gentle touch — and you possess both. It's an honor to walk these books to the finish line with you!

Finally, a personal note to my family and the families of all my co-authors. Thank you for the time you've given us to squirrel away at our writing desks, or the time we've spent on social media preparing our audiences for this book. Thank you for your supportive words of encouragement when we needed it. And mostly, thank you for believing our stories matter.

INTRODUCTION

Introduction

I can't remember the first time I publicly used the phrase *step into your brave* — but what I do recall is the immediate reaction to it.

People responded to it viscerally; they felt a connection because it conjured up their own memories of when they had to find the courage to do something when it was hard, scary, or even dangerous.

This collaborative book is the second in a series we're publishing at LIGHTbeamers. Our first book, *Elevate Your Voice*, was a number-one Amazon bestseller, and the stories inside challenged readers to find ways to use their own stories to elevate their voices in the world.

I daresay the same is true of this book. Our call to you, the reader, is to find ways to be courageous and do the things that scare you or feel hard. We are inviting you to step into your brave.

Turns out, leading this book series project for a second time required me to step into my brave. I had to battle doubts about whether we would be able to repeat the magic we experienced the first time around with our authors, and whether this book would "measure up" to our first book's success. Like you, I have my own set of doubts and fears . . . and I have to find my own courage to navigate the hard and scary things.

I was a guest on a podcast recently when the host said to me, "April, you are putting yourself out there in such big ways. How do you find the courage to do it?"

Courage??

It took me a second to reply.

I don't see myself as innately courageous.

When I'm moving things forward in my life or business, I'm not consciously tapping into my "courage" or giving myself internal pep talks about being "courageous." If I'm not actively looking for my courage before I step into my brave, then how am I able to do it? How did I get here, writing and publishing books and leading other women to do the same?

Lean into this with me. . . *I'm not thinking about myself in those moments. I'm thinking about my audience.*

Introduction

My work at LIGHTbeamers is to equip and empower women to tell their stories. To become brilliant storytellers. Yet the very first thing I teach them is my number-one rule of storytelling: *Know your audience. Know who you are talking to*!

If I thought for one second about myself and how "courageous" I was being, I'd throw up. I would most certainly freeze with fear, and I would never do the "big" things I've done in my life.

In other words, *I get out of my own way*.

The success of this book isn't about me or the other authors you'll meet here. The success of this book is about *you*, our reader.

We stepped into our brave not because of what sharing our stories would do for us, but rather because of what it might do for you.

On the pages that follow, you'll find a bevy of stories we hope will reach into your heart and soul and touch you in a way that moves you to action. Stories of loss, trauma, pain, rebirth, redemption, freedom, and so much more.

The stories we share here are not just our stories — they are yours, too!

This is what I know to be true about storytelling: When one person is courageous enough to show up and share their story, the ripple effect is activated. That story reaches someone else, and then they find their own hidden batch of courage and do something impactful in their life, even if it seems small and insignificant. Then, their action gets noticed by someone else and they are inspired in new ways as well. You see what's happening? The ripple reaches far beyond that first point of impact.

In most cases, we'll never know the ripple effect created by writing this book and sharing our individual stories. But we trust it's there, regardless.

My hope for you is that by reading these stories you will be inspired into action in your own unique and powerful ways. You will keep the ripple going. It's bold to believe that's possible, so with that in mind, we *are* stepping into our brave!

And you will step into yours!

And others will do the same.

Ripple
Ripple Ripple
Ripple Ripple Ripple

Here's to initiating that ripple. Enjoy the read.

XO,
April

Chapter 1

LISTEN TO YOUR HEART

April Adams Pertuis

"The heart doesn't care about distance; it beats with love no matter what."

His hair fell to the ground, mixing with the dust and debris already gathered inside the carport. I realized this was a preview of what was to come. Using his rickety hair trimmers, I hovered over the top of his head to finish off the patches he'd missed earlier while attempting to do the job himself. I thought about the ways in which I'd judged him for his weakness, his inability to kick bad habits or commit to anything substantial and meaningful. His addictions had always come first and clouded his ability to be emotionally available. As I stood there in his carport, cutting his hair that was beginning to show the ravages of cancer, I wondered, *Where are your addictions now? They certainly aren't here, cutting your hair.*

Dad's health had been declining for the past four years. But in reality, it had been declining for decades. He had started smoking at age twelve; he had been a heavy drinker for as long as I could remember; his favorite food was anything southern, smothered, and fried. Dad didn't play in the realm of "limits" . . . His life's motto was "Screw the rules and have fun doing it." A perpetual life-of-the-party kind of guy, he played hard, lived fast, and was oblivious to some of the debris left in his path.

My mom divorced him when I was 17. He had a string of other relationships but none of them lasted. While he was always a good provider, at least for himself, his career was topsy turvy with long stints as an entrepreneur that ultimately ended with him becoming someone else's employee. As he aged and as his health declined, gainful employment became a challenge. He took social security much sooner than he would have liked and was living on a very fixed and limited income. While he'd enjoyed much financial success in his life, he arrived in his 70's without a lot to show for it.

How he approached his health was no exception.

These last four years were the culmination of more than sixty years of living without any regard to consequences. And when his health began its downward turn, it spiraled fast. Before his cancer diagnosis, Dad was battling the effects of chronic obstructive pulmonary disease (COPD) and congestive heart failure. I had been living in South Carolina, which was a healthy thousand-mile distance from the daily ins and outs of Dad's life. I would rush home to Texas anytime my sister called to let me know Dad's health had turned serious and he was hospitalized. The year before I moved back to Texas, I had crisscrossed back and forth from South Carolina to Texas six times. . . each time a hospitalization warranting my emergency trip. Now I was back in Texas, having moved my immediate family so that I could be closer to my parents and siblings, and be more available to help with Dad's needs. It was a new role I was having to sort myself into, because I'd never fully developed a relationship with my dad that leaned toward daily interaction.

Ours had always been a long-distance relationship.

When I was a kid growing up, the distance was less physical and more emotional. Though my dad was present in the home, he left for work before I got out of bed, and made his daily pitstop at the local bar before he made his way home at night, often after our dinner dishes were put away and I was already hiding away in my room like most kids. I don't have many memories of us gathering around the kitchen table to discuss our day, or making breakfast together before heading off to school, or watching family TV shows and laughing at the hilarity of the story line.

I don't recall him teaching me how to do anything like how to shoot a gun, plant a garden, or build a fort out of sticks. Dad never seemed interested in that kind of stuff. His focus was on work, social life, and his friends. I never felt like I was my dad's first priority. Instead, I felt like his family was secondary.

If it didn't involve a weekend getaway to our family lake house or social gatherings at our home (my parents threw a lot of parties), I don't have many significant imprints of how Dad fit into my life as a child. My strongest and fondest memory of Dad from those days was when he spent one summer teaching me how to water-ski at the lake house. But even then, Dad was a hard-ass. He'd look at me with a cigarette hanging out of his mouth, sitting at the steering wheel of the boat, and say, "April, get your ass in the water. It's time you learn how to water-ski." And when I'd fall down and beg to get back into the boat, he'd say, "Nah. You're not done. The only way you're going to get it is if we drag you all over this lake until you get up." Of course, once I finally got up, I loved the feeling of gliding across the water. And Dad got more kicks out of tossing the boat from left to right to force me outside the wake. When I learned to cross the wake without falling, his next trick was to speed up to test the boundaries of how fast I could go. Dad didn't play inside the box. I learned that at an early age.

In high school, the distance between us was slightly more physical. I attended a prestigious all-girls high school, where I lived on campus as a boarding student. In college, the distance continued as I enjoyed the autonomy and freedom that came from living on my own and making my own decisions. I was heavily involved in campus leadership and dove headfirst into sorority life. I was going on dates, making new friends, and discovering new things in my area of study. It was an exciting time and I loved all of it. I wasn't exactly craving input from my parents, nor was I actively seeking their support — I was enjoying the ability to flex my independence and test my own boundaries and limits. Nonetheless, as I look back on those years, I don't remember my dad ever coming to the college campus for a visit, even though I was only an hour away. My mom would come for visits, take me out to dinner or lunch, buy me a round of groceries to stock my dorm room fridge, and stuff a few extra bucks into my hand when she left. But I don't remember my dad ever doing that. Instead, Dad would wait for me to come home for a visit, and when I did, he'd throw a party. There was always a group gathering at his house for a fish fry, or he'd invite me to come hang out with the boys at the bar. That was how Dad wanted to spend time with me, and I often obliged, because I knew it was the only way I could spend time with him.

After college, I put even more distance between Dad and me when I accepted a job in Arkansas, and later moved across the country to the Carolinas after I got married. After the birth of both of my children, my mom visited immediately, but it was months before my dad met his grandchildren, and only because I flew home to Texas with my new baby for a visit.

At every stage of my life, Dad played more of a supporting role to my mother's leadership, guidance, and influence. Yet, anytime I was around him, there was always laughter and good times as we celebrated over good food and good drinks.

For more than twenty-five years this was the status of our relationship: a phone call occasionally (and only if I initiated it) and a personal visit whenever I happened to be passing through town. And always, our time together was mostly cordial. Although I didn't always agree with my dad, or his lifestyle, we never argued or had a contentious relationship. Dad was just Dad. Somewhere along the way I had accepted that this was who he was, and I made sure it didn't affect me in my daily life.

The truth is, I really didn't know my dad. I wasn't aware of how he moved throughout his day, how he liked his coffee, or what some of his fears, worries, and doubts were as an adult. I knew him only from a very high level, a 360-degree aerial view. I knew what he did for a living, I knew he favored Miller Lite beer, and I knew the people he mentioned in his stories were all guys he hung out with at the local beer joint. These were his buddies. His posse. The people he did life with. I hadn't been a part of his day-to-day life, and I wasn't privy to his affairs. It was a complete divergence from my relationship with my mother. She was my personal confidante.

She was an open book — she shared her stories with me and let me know how her mistakes and misfortune had shaped her. She shared those lessons with me in hopes of shortcutting some of my own series of falling down. For years, I took comfort and solace in my relationship with my mother and was grateful for her influence in my life. Her presence made it easier to accept the gaping holes left by my dad.

When Dad's health began to decline, he unknowingly started weaving himself into my life in more significant ways. I was praying for him. I was checking in on him more frequently. I was discussing him around the dinner table with my husband and kids. I talked about "Big Daddy" and gave them weekly updates. Suddenly, the thousand-mile distance between South Carolina and Texas, which acutely represented the figurative distance between us, felt hard. For all those years, I had relished the distance I had put between myself and my family. I loved living on the East Coast and was proud of the life I had built there with my husband and kids. I had raised kids without much help from family, other than the times my mom would come to rescue us and watch the kids while my husband and I took an adult vacation or simply spend the weekend with us and immerse herself in our life for four days.

So it made no sense to me when thoughts began swirling in my head, nudging me to explore the idea of moving back to Texas. We had built an amazing life, were completely rooted in our community, and were living in a dream house on top of a mountain with long-range views. Our careers were cranking, and our kids were excelling at school and fully involved with their gaggle of friends. Why on earth would we disrupt this nirvana?

Sometimes God asks you to do things your selfish ego doesn't want to do.

The thoughts in my head became more pronounced as God continued to nudge me back to Texas. The housing market was going crazy, and we could make a pretty penny from the sale of our house. Our kids loved our increasingly frequent trips home to Texas and enjoyed learning more about their Texas roots with each visit. I enjoyed the time I got to spend with old friends and my siblings. All of my husband's family was also in Texas. His dad was the same age as mine, and he was beginning to show serious effects of aging. He was about to undergo hip replacement surgery, and doctors were concerned about early stages of dementia.

"April, your family needs you," I could hear God whisper in my ear.

In the spring of 2017, we made the decision to put our house on the market. We flew to Texas over spring break to house hunt. We timed our move perfectly so our kids could complete the school year. Our son was finishing elementary school. We thought moving him now wouldn't be as disruptive, since he'd be starting a new school anyway by entering middle school. We felt God's urging more consistently and were trying to be obedient while also convincing ourselves this was all our idea and a really great decision based on where we were in our life. Decisions like this are so much easier to make when you feel like you are in control of them. We justified it at every turn. It made sense, the timing was right, and our family needed us. We would sacrifice our big, beautiful, precious life in South Carolina to embrace a new adventure, be more present with family, and enjoy the healthy profit we'd make on selling our house. At every turn, we kept finding all the reasons why this was a smart move.

But make no mistake about it: at the very nucleus of this decision was Dad. I was embarking on reshuffling every single aspect of my life for a man who'd never gone out of his way to make room for me. And deep down, that fact took root and I began living a story I had secretly been crafting for forty years. When I arrived in Texas, I brought with me a U-Haul full of judgment and bitterness that I would soon unleash.

The first six months of our new life in Texas was a tearstained blur. I was a mess. It was like my entire physical body was rejecting this transplant. On the outside, I was smiling and joyful — embracing family dinners with my dad and sister, and racing up the highway to visit my mom as much as possible. A plane ride no longer separated us! But behind closed doors I couldn't even think about the move without bursting into tears. I was resentful almost immediately upon arrival. This wasn't my fault. . . This was God's fault. Why had he urged me to move? This was the most ridiculous thing we'd ever done. It wasn't just me, either — the kids were a mess, too. Moving to a new state and new neighborhood, and entering brand-new schools with zero friends was overwhelming and caused a lot of anxiety to fill the house. I feared we'd made a big mistake, one we might not be able to recover from. Through it all, I did my best to hide my feelings and focus instead on taking care of Dad.

At first, gathering with Dad on a regular basis was fun. It was like we were both embracing the opportunity to get to know each other again — after all, the distance between us was real. I spent many afternoons visiting with him, telling him about my career, and sharing some of the interesting projects I was working on with clients. Dad would shower me with praise and tell me how proud he was of me and the dedication I showed to my work. Dad also showed eagerness to get to know the kids, his grandchildren, better. He'd ask them about school and extracurricular activities and seemed to honestly take note of their different personalities. He'd crack jokes with them and always liked it when I brought them over for a visit.

We fell into a nice rhythm of weekly lunch dates out at some of his favorite restaurants. We discussed politics or a new movie he had watched the night before, or — and this was one of his favorite ways to pass the time — he'd recount stories from his youth. Some of them were hysterical accounts of some of the stupid shenanigans he'd gotten himself into, and others were more nostalgic tales of "how the world used to be."

And always, he'd find a way to creep in a crude joke. Deep down, he knew those yanked my chain, because they were always off-color, condescending, or full of sexual innuendos (sometimes all three). I'd chastise him for being inappropriate, and he'd just cock his head back and laugh. He knew I hated his jokes, and he loved poking me with them.

Rather quickly, my regular visits became a rude invitation to see how inaccurate I had been to assume the physical distance between us all those years was synonymous with "acceptance." As I observed him, I silently racked up more evidence of how ill-equipped he was to navigate this stage of his life. A serious diagnosis of COPD from more than sixty years of chain smoking meant he desperately needed assistance from an oxygen tank that he refused to wear. Congestive heart failure was a result of all the fat-drenched foods he loved so much. I worked hard to insert my green juice, vegetarian-leaning lifestyle into his daily routine. I'd make a healthy dinner and bring him a container full of leftovers. Weeks later, I'd find it shoved into the back of his refrigerator, covered in mold. I suggested he wear his oxygen more by luring him with words of encouragement about how much less winded he'd get just walking to his truck. He challenged me by saying, "I do wear it, April. I don't like wearing it when I have visitors, but I do wear it when I'm here by myself." I'd make a surprise visit the next day and open the front door only to find him asleep in his chair, the oxygen hose still lying in the same position it was in the day before.

At every turn, I used his lifestyle and choices as demerits on my secret scale of approval. My judgment meter sharpened. My disgust was hard to hide. I openly challenged him during heated discussions about his decisions. He'd end it by saying, "I'm not going to argue with you, April," and quickly change the subject. When that tactic didn't work, I'd secretly remove things from his home or pretend to accidentally forget to buy things on his grocery order to prioritize my way of living over his.

My sharp edges continued to emerge even while Dad seemed to need me more every day. As he became more accustomed to my visits, he ramped up his requests. There were trips to the pharmacy, grocery order pickups, calls to the billing department of one of his many doctors and specialists. As if that weren't enough, he would call me multiple times a week with some random question about computers or ask me to research something he'd seen advertised on one of those atrocious as-seen-on-TV infomercials they show late at night. My agitation grew with each request. Why was he bothering me with this junk? Didn't he realize we had more pressing issues to worry about, like how he was going to manage his health and continue to live independently down the road? Behind the scenes I was already projecting what I imagined the next few years would be like. I called around to assisted-living facilities and inquired about home health care, predicting those days were soon upon us. I was in a place of massive assumptions, and his seeming inattentiveness to these important details wore on my very last nerve.

When I spilled my guts to a friend who worked in senior living care one day, she stopped me dead in my tracks when she pointed out, "April, these are his choices. He's a grown man and has been living his life without you all of these years. Clearly none of this seems to bother him, so why are you letting it bother you?"

She was right. Getting up close and personal with Dad's lifestyle didn't entitle me to criticize it and try to reorder everything to suit my tastes. I was letting everything about Dad's lifestyle, his daily choices, and his vision for the future dictate my own level of calm and serenity. I was overcompensating in the relationship, and taking things so far to the other side, I had become the type of daughter I didn't want to be. I was struggling in my new role here, and I was completely out of balance with navigating my own life while attempting to reestablish the role of a dutiful daughter.

Like most things, life has a way of handing you a road map when you least expect it.

For months, Dad had been complaining of not being able to swallow easily. Food would get trapped, and he'd have to throw up to clear his airway. My sister and I grew increasingly concerned, so we made an appointment with an ear, nose, and throat (ENT) doctor. He ordered a scope procedure in which Dad had to be hospitalized and put to sleep. In typical Dad fashion, he had the nurses in hysterics in the room where he waited to be wheeled back for the procedure. He was snappy with my sister and me because he hadn't eaten since the night before, adhering to strict doctor's orders (for once) not to have anything to eat or drink for twelve hours before receiving anesthesia. Dad didn't miss a meal, so he turned any sort of minor restriction like this into a major complaint.

"Y'all hurry up and wheel my ass back there so you can get this scope job done and I can get me something to eat," he barked at the attending nurses in his best back-country Texas drawl, like a foreman herding cattle on a ranch.

There was never, ever any talk about what might be causing the entrapment in his esophagus. He never openly discussed his fears or thoughts with us. Rather, he asked us where we were going to go to lunch when this was all over.

Later, sitting in the waiting room with the ENT specialist, he revealed what my sister and I had feared.

CANCER

In that moment, everything changed. Suddenly, there was a full schedule of doctors' appointments, ports being installed, chemo education and visits, and a rigid schedule of daily radiation. Dad and I became a team. I oversaw much of this, because my sister was working a demanding job as a high school principal. Since I owned my own business, I had more flexibility to be present throughout the day.

In between all of this, I was trying to manage my own family and career, meet the needs of my children, and continue to heal my heartbreak over our cross-country move. I was nursing a broken heart while having my heart broken again, watching my dad being pumped full of toxic juice for hours each week in hopes that these toxins would be powerful enough to kill the cancer, but not so powerful that it would kill him in the process. Having been the daughter who'd spent most of her life enjoying the distance of our relationship, I was getting a PhD in Dad and every crevice of his body.

Everything they say about cancer and chemotherapy is true. It's a nightmare. It's a beast. It's the scariest battle I have ever witnessed in my life. It robs you of all of your time, joy, comforts, and independence. You stop being you and become only a cancer patient. It's the only title you have. It becomes your full-time job.

With each passing week, Dad became weaker and weaker. His appetite completely disappeared, and for months the only thing he ate were vanilla milkshakes from Chick-fil-A. At first, I was determined to help him beat cancer by feeding him good food and getting him back to health. I was delusional, of course, because this seventy-seven-year-old man was not about to give up cheeseburgers and steaks to adopt my clean-eating lifestyle. Plus, the milkshakes were a blessing, because they were the only thing he could keep down. His weight plummeted. I'd never seen my dad weigh less than 275 pounds, but he lost roughly 90 pounds throughout his treatment.

Slowly, his jovial disposition disappeared. He no longer had energy to go have a beer with the boys. In fact, he quit drinking and smoking altogether — a day I never thought I'd see. It was all he could do to get out of his chair and shuffle the mere six steps to his dining room table to suck down his milkshake. After months of this, I asked him, "How can you still drink those? Aren't you sick of them yet?" To which he replied, "No, sweetheart. They taste so good." He'd cock his head back and cackle out one of his trademark belly laughs.

One day at the chemo clinic, I watched him step up on the scale like he'd done every other visit. He was hunched over, gripping the handlebars to steady himself and keep upright. Sitting off to the side, I studied him. His skin was gray. His face was gaunt. His eyes were glassy. He was a shell of a man with hardly any life left inside. I walked behind him as he shuffled slowly to the examination room to wait for the doctor. It was only a few steps from the scale to the room, but I am certain it took us ten minutes to reach the threshold. Watching him from behind, I thought, *This is a dead man walking.* I couldn't fathom how he was still with us.

I gotta hand it to him: even on his worst days, like this one, and even when his doctors continued to give his prognosis in terms of months, doing their best to prepare us for what was coming, Dad never wavered in his resolve to get on the other side of cancer. "It's going to get better. I just gotta hold on until I can turn this corner." When the doctors would talk in pragmatic, the-odds-aren't-good terms, he'd tell them to shut the hell up. "Where is your faith?" he'd ask them. This from a man I've never known to be religious, much less evangelical, yet he was preaching to these doctors that faith and God would bring him through.

Three months after he completed his last chemo treatment, I pulled up to his apartment and found him sitting outside in his carport, enjoying the cooler weather and soaking up the beautiful day while the cleaning lady I had sent over was inside cleaning his apartment. He looked good. Really good, actually. He was a far cry from the dead man walking

I'd seen months earlier. It seemed Dad had done exactly what he believed. He'd beat cancer — despite everything, he was on the mend. His bright smile was back. The color in his skin had returned. And his sick sense of humor was back on display. I halfway couldn't believe it myself. As someone who's relied heavily on her faith during my own tough times in life, I found Dad's unwavering belief that he beat cancer awe-inspiring, to say the least.

Four months later, we got the news that his cancer had returned with a vengeance. Dad had been complaining of severe back pain. Turns out, the pain was warranted, because the cancer had spread to his spine and lungs. This time, it was terminal. Sitting with the doctors that day, Dad looked at me and said, "Well, sweetie, we gave it a good run!'" We both knew a second round of chemo and radiation wasn't something we were willing to do. And Dad's doctors agreed. They told us the stats and predictions, and none of them were odds we were willing to bet on. Before we left, the doctor gave us what I think was some of the best advice we received throughout this whole ordeal.

"Sign up for hospice now," the oncologist said. "Don't wait until the end. Use their services now. It will make whatever time he has left much more bearable."

By late that afternoon, a hospice representative was sitting on Dad's couch handing me paperwork to sign. Within two days, he was set up on a full schedule of home visits that included nurses, volunteers, and chaplains. Dad welcomed all of it. He didn't resist any of the influx of people in his home. By the grace of God, he did what doctors suggested. Dad took to his hospice nurse right away. Whatever she suggested, he signed up for it. He even agreed to have meals delivered to his home once a day by local volunteers. Of course, he didn't eat them — but he was putting up a good front for those who were bending over backward trying to help him. He was appreciative of all of it.

One day, I noticed a fine white dust accumulating around Dad's beloved easy chair. I'd been noticing it for weeks, but on this day, the accumulation seemed substantial. It dawned on me that it was literally *his dust*. His skin was flaking and falling away while he sat and slept.

He's literally turning to dust, I thought.

The promises of the Bible — from dust to dust — were playing out right in front of my eyes. Time passes painfully slow when you're watching someone wither away like that. There were many days I prayed Dad would die suddenly — that the Lord would just take him and eliminate this extended misery. *A heart attack would be convenient. We already know his heart is failing, so just take him!*

My bargaining and reasoning with God only sent me looking in the mirror. *Who am I to wish this man dead? Why? So that it will be easier for me?* It was during these reflection times that I began to see so clearly why God had nudged me to move back to Texas to care for a dad with whom I had so little connection. In a weirdly profound way, I began to realize God had sent me here to be an eyewitness to this particular death. I began documenting some of my experiences in a brand-new journal I had purchased for the purpose of writing my hopes and aspirations. Instead, God asked me to write stories about Dad.

Dad asked us to take him to the beach for one last visit to the water. The Texas coast was an easy three-hour drive away. For months, Dad kept asking us to make the plans, take off work, and clear our calendars for the trip. He wanted to have lunch at a favorite seafood place on the bay, then drive over to see the beach one last time. My sister and I were always juggling Dad's requests with the demands of our own busy lives, and regrettably, by the time we organized this trip, Dad was in worse shape. Once we arrived in Corpus Christi, we stopped for lunch and proceeded to do what Dad loved the most — we ate fried food and ordered a round of stout drinks. When our drinks arrived, my sister and I looked at each other knowingly and ordered another round. Despite the hustle of getting this day trip in order, we settled into the laid-back vibe of the restaurant. All around us were men and women dressed professionally, making business deals over gumbo and seeing each other off with a handshake. Their lunches were quick, and tables around us were turning over with new guests while the three of us lingered over our meal as if time would never run out. We knew this would be the last time we'd ever take Dad out to eat.

By the end of lunch, Dad was exhausted. The trip had already taken a toll on his energy, and he told us as we helped him to the truck to forget the beach. He just wanted to hit the road and go home. My sister and I protested. We were right on the bay, and offered up a compromise: we'd just drive across the street and let him get out and take in the ocean smells. We parked his truck as close to the water as we could get and helped him out into the parking lot. He stood at the water's edge and took in the mixture of salt, fish, and sea smells. We lined up in front of the seawall and turned Dad around so that the water was behind him. I pulled out my iPhone and took a selfie of the three of us. It was the last photo of us together.

On the ride home, Dad handed me a yellow notebook. With my sister driving and me sitting in the back, he began giving me instructions from the front passenger seat.

He gave specific details on how he wanted us to celebrate his life after he was gone. He was adamant about not having a funeral or burial. Instead he wanted to be cremated. He invited us to throw a party out on the lake. He wanted us to rent pontoon boats, pack an ice chest full of beer, and celebrate with country music and sunshine. He dictated a specific playlist of songs he wanted us to blast while we spread his ashes across the water. "I Love This Bar" by Toby Keith was on his list. That was so Dad! Another one was "Prop Me Up Beside the Jukebox (If I Die)." The last one on his list — "Amazing Grace."

By spring 2020, it was a daily concern what condition I might find Dad in when I went to his house for my daily check-ins. I'd been preparing for months for the very real possibility I might find him dead in his chair one day. When the Covid-19 pandemic rolled around, we took drastic measures to keep Dad inside and limited his visitors. Limiting his independence and social capacity was his last straw. By mid-April, he was declining rapidly, with noticeable changes at each daily visit. My sister and I consulted with our lifeline — his hospice caregivers. We knew we needed a plan of action for getting him round-the-clock care. They made arrangements for Dad to get into a skilled nursing facility for a five-day "respite" care visit. It was temporary — just five days. It was long enough for dad to get twenty-four-hour care and for my sister and I to catch our breath. We knew we were close — though with cancer you never really know. It could be two weeks or it could be two months.

The situation at skilled nursing facilities during the height of the pandemic added a quadruple layer of complexity and insanity to an already excruciating circumstance. We could drop Dad off at the front door, but we wouldn't be allowed to walk him in or help him get settled into his room. And, we wouldn't be able to visit at all during his five-day stay. Our only connection would be communication from the hospice workers, who'd be able to give us daily reports by phone.

We didn't need them.

Dad called daily asking us to come get him and bring him home. He reported he was getting absentee care and that he was spending his entire days alone. I'd hang up from these calls in tears, praying, "Please, Lord! We just need him to get through the next couple of days!" Those were the longest days of my life. Though Dad was only a few miles away, the distance felt like a million miles. For the first time in my entire life, I felt the gravity and pain of this distance from my dad. I was so ready to get him back home, and within those few days, my sister and I sorted a plan where we'd take turns caring for him around the clock. It wasn't going to be easy, juggling the needs of our own lives and families, but we saw no other way. We were already seeing how awful the alternative of long-term care would be, especially in the madness of the pandemic, and we wouldn't do that to him (or to us!). We would take turns seeing to his needs and wait for the end.

When Dad came home on the fifth day, he was nearly unrecognizable. His speech was slurred, his eyes were bulging, and he was slumped over in his wheelchair. We'd already made all sorts of special accommodations inside his apartment, including having a hospital bed placed right by his easy chair in the living room. The hospice nurse was there with us and helped us get him cleaned up and into the bed. My sister was taking the first shift, and after Dad fell asleep for the night, I went home. I promised her I'd come back first thing in the morning with a strong cup of coffee and offer her a break. That next morning, when I was about to leave my house, my sister called crying. *"April, he's gone."*

Dad died in his sleep, resting peacefully in his home. He'd been returned to us. The distance had been eliminated, and he was able to let go.

I've judged myself harshly for sending him for those five days of respite care. I've played the insidious game of "should've, would've, could've" over and over in my head. It breaks my heart to think Dad spent his last days alive in that cold place, alone, as a result of the heinous wreckage created by the pandemic. In his dying days, I created more distance between us.

Distance had long played a role in my relationship with my dad. So had judgment. On that April morning, I could only recall the thousands of intimate details I'd discovered about him since moving back to Texas. The last three years of being with him almost daily had healed an ocean-wide distance of emotional separation and allowed me to see him for who he really was. I no longer saw a man who was weak and unable to love his family. My fierce judgment of him had been replaced with deep appreciation for his uniqueness and independence. These are qualities I greatly admire in others and try hard to exhibit myself. Dad lived life uniquely and authentically his way. He didn't cater to other people's rules or agendas.

I still find myself driving by his old apartment. I feel connected to the memories of him. Not so much the ones of my childhood but those of his last three years on earth. I've noticed I'm much less quick to judge others and more accepting of who they are. I also celebrate people more now for being different, marching to the beat of their own drum, and maybe even doing things that are socially unacceptable. After all, who's making the rules? I ask. I'm grateful for these lessons, even though they came at a great cost.

God always gets it right. He didn't call me home so that I could witness Dad's death. He called me home so I could experience Dad while he was still alive. I may not have gotten the best years of his life, but the memories of taking care of him leading up to his death will be seared on my heart forever.

I realize that distance wasn't the accurate measurement of my relationship with Dad. It was willingness and openness. The heart doesn't care about distance; it beats with love no matter what. I willingly moved in order to be closer to him and care for him. And in doing so, I opened myself to the possibility of loving Dad in a new way. It was never the textbook version of a daddy-daughter relationship, but then again, Dad wasn't exactly your textbook kind of guy. To fully know and appreciate people, you have to take down your own ideal of how it "should" be, and meet people where they are.

Months later when we scattered Dad's ashes across the lake, the people who were there, celebrating him, were those who mattered the most — his family. I daresay none of us had an easy relationship with Dad. My mom and my siblings all had their own uncharacteristic relationship with him, yet there we were . . . all of us together, drinking Miller Lite beer, belting out country tunes, and soaking up the Texas sunshine, hosting the party Dad had planned and living it out exactly as he wished.

And I'm pretty sure dad was enjoying all of it from heaven. I imagine him sitting at the helm of the boat — wearing his ball cap turned around backward, the sun hitting his tan skin and reflecting off his bright smile. Right on cue, he'd hit the throttle to try to throw us outside the wake and force us to go on a ride we didn't expect.

ABOUT THE AUTHOR
APRIL ADAMS PERTUIS

April Adams Pertuis has been a storyteller since she was a little girl, hiding out in her room writing secret poems and scribbling stories on the wood slats underneath her bed. An extreme sense of curiosity led her to ask a lot of questions when talking to people, wondering what secret story was hiding inside. It's no surprise that that keen interest led her to journalism school and a lengthy career as a television journalist, video producer, and brand storyteller.

In 2014, frustration over the stories being shared on social media led her on a quest to go deeper with her work. Desiring to make an impact on women's stories, she created LIGHTbeamers. Today, April leads the LIGHTbeamers Community, full of women who are curious about their own stories, and helps them excavate the layers of their stories through various online courses and coaching programs. She also hosts the Inside Story podcast, the Storytelling

Symposium, and is the co-creator of the LIGHTbeamers *She Gets Published* Author Program, all of which give women a platform from which to share their stories with the world.

When April isn't dreaming up ways to equip and empower women through storytelling, she is hanging out with her husband and two kids, traveling somewhere in the mountains, or soaking up the good Texas sunshine and eating tacos.

Learn more about April and her work on pages 252-255.

Chapter 2

GATHER YOUR COURAGE

Kristi Koehler

"Don't give fear more strength than it deserves."

FACING REALITY

As time passed, the weight of the chains got heavier, and the pressures of my situation came crashing down, suffocating my soul. I was naïve to think I was hiding my brokenness; to some people, the pain was obvious.

What started out as a typical sports-filled Saturday morning turned into a real awakening. I can still remember that day vividly, the day my soul awoke and breathed life again. Focused on the sound of children's voices screaming for the basketball and parents suggesting their child's next move, I was startled by the touch of a hand on my left thigh. I turned to see a mom from my daughter's team, someone I had rarely spoken to.

"I hope I'm not overstepping any boundaries," she said. "I can see you are hurting, and I want to let you know that I am here for you. My husband and I had problems in the past, and we are doing awesome now. I know a great counselor, if you're interested."

The world around me stopped as her words soaked in. All I can remember is taking in a huge gasp of air — like people do in the movies when they are brought back from near death. I took in so much air, I am surprised my lungs did not rupture. Despite my involuntary, telltale response, I reassured her, "I'm fine!" — something I had gotten good at telling myself.

The rest of the game was a blur as my sensations began to return. The depth to which I had become numb became evident when I got in my car, one I had had for years, put my hands on the steering wheel, and noticed bumps. *Bumps?* I sat there for a bit just getting reacquainted with my senses — running my fingers repeatedly along the steering wheel bumps and listening to the sounds of the environment coming to life around me.

MARRIAGE GONE WRONG

As far back as I had witnessed, marriages on both sides of my family were built around an arrangement that there was a "man of the house" and a woman's voice carried little, and sometimes no, weight. You did what the man said . . . period! As a child, after years of observing marriage within my family, I promised myself a different kind of love.

Although my marriage was profoundly different, on this day, I woke up drowning in a relationship far from the one I had dreamed about. Repeating the marriage cycle I had witnessed growing up, I realized I was craving the kind of love displayed in 1 Corinthians 13:4-7.

The last thing I wanted was for my soul to die while my body was still very much alive. I had to make a decision, but divorce was not something I believed in. I had to find the warrior in me willing to fight to end this vicious cycle and gain the strength to remove the weight of these "chains." My two daughters deserved to experience healthy love and true friendships — and so did I, for that matter.

SAVING MYSELF

There is a reason flight attendants tell you, "If you are traveling with small children, please put your own oxygen mask on first before putting one on your children." My gut instinct is to protect my children first and foremost. The flight attendants were right, though: I had to save myself if I had any hopes of saving my girls. When I realized the life had been sucked out of my soul, I had to resuscitate myself, take my health into my own hands, and gain ownership of my life. I had to own my faults, and focus on repairing my mental and physical well-being. If it meant letting go and forgiving those I did not think deserved it, I had to do it so that my daughters and I could live. . . really live. I had to stop lying to myself.

A counselor once told me, "Nice people lie, but the people they lie to the most is themselves." I was 100 percent guilty, and it was time to stop. That meant I also had to stop indirectly lying to others by making excuses for my failing marriage. It was time to talk to the reflection in the mirror and search down to my core for truth. Time to stop defending what did not deserve defending. First things first, I had to stop lying to myself and face my fears . . . all of them. Oh boy, talk about opening a can of worms!

We can all be good at hiding how crazy our lives are and good at hiding our hurts and fears. Like ducks, we may seem cool and chill on the surface, but underneath we're paddling like hell to stay afloat. Or as a coworker once told me, in his French-Canadian accent, after he listened to me respond to a customer's call in the midst of an insanely crazy day, "You just picked up that phone and answered it so calm and collected, like nothing was going on in the world around you. If I didn't know any better, I would have thought you were spending a relaxing day at the beach. How do you do that?" Learning to function in a highly chaotic environment while remaining positive is what we mothers do best. We can't always count on someone to notice our pains and tap our leg to wake us up; we can be surprisingly good actors.

TIME FOR COUNSELING

Divorce was foreign to me, and I had no idea how to navigate around it. Not many of my close friends had been through it.

Feeling so alone, I decided I could no longer fight this fight without help. I could no longer do it on my own.

I found no shame in going to counseling. There was so much to overcome when divorce became inevitable — my failures, my faults, his faults, religious beliefs, letting people down, losing friends, all the tentacles of divorce but most importantly the potential effects on my baby girls. I had to ask myself, was this the kind of marriage I wished for them to witness as an example? What was this teaching them about love and how to love others? Bottom line, our role as parents is to teach our children love, respect, and how to be kind and caring human beings.

"The apple doesn't fall far from the tree," I have often heard in reference to children turning out like their parents or following in their footsteps. If those thoughts alone did not give me the strength to face the hardships of divorce for their hope and my peace, I do not know what did. I was ready!

Or was I? No time was ever going to be easy. I had to find the courage to be brave for all of us.

FEAR SHOWS UP

Fear is a con artist.

We give it more strength than it deserves.

Looking back now, I realize that one of the most important things I learned in college was that fear is one of the most accomplished con artists on this earth. At some point — or perhaps several points — in our lives, we're going to feel fear. Whether we're reacting to a physical threat or we're anxious about something, we all have to face it.

The moment I realized I needed to take control of my fears was when I had a full-on panic attack simply walking up a flight of stairs. A small opening between the wall and the steps allowed you to see the bottom floor. Those of you who have an extreme fear of heights can relate: the fear just hits you! Fear immediately told me I was going to slip through that opening and fall straight to the bottom floor. *Seriously — what the what?!*

After my heart rate normalized and my breath calmed, I could not help but laugh at myself. Why had I not seen it before? Fear was full of shit, fresh ground fertilizer, a perpetual liar that I had been buying into for years! There was no way my Koehler butt was going to fit through that three-inch opening. That is the moment I took a stance to overcome fear and all its ridiculousness. I was no longer going to allow this absurdity to control my life. Since that day I have pushed myself out of my comfort zone and into moments where I have learned how to own my fears. I find this much easier when I have the right people by my side to push me to the edge of my brave.

REACHING NEW HEIGHTS

While overcoming my fears, I became addicted to the incredible views from the top of 14ers. A 14er is any mountain with a peak greater than fourteen thousand feet. This was no small feat for a big chicken! In an effort to challenge myself, I decided to join a group of friends on a mission to climb 14ers in Colorado on our annual summer trip. For three years, hiking with the same group of friends, I did a great job of hiding my internal struggles — that is, until one particular climb. I came upon a very narrow catwalk with thirteen thousand feet of drop-off on either side.

All I could do was start laughing. My friends looked around a bit, confused, trying to figure out what they had missed. Continuing to laugh, I said, "I guess now is a good time to tell you that I am deathly afraid of heights. I don't think I can go any farther." I then internalized the fear and said to myself, *Face your fears, sister. That is why we're here, remember?* I agreed to trudge on, although like a big scaredy-cat, I shielded my peripheral vision and focused on the path that had been worn down by those before me.

On our journey through bravery, which many before us have taken, we don't always make it to the summit or accomplish everything we set out to do, and sometimes the struggle is even greater than we signed up for. Sometimes we get really close yet still never find the gallantry to make it. Unfortunately, I have come up short on courage and failed many times, and fourteen thousand feet in the air appears to be where these lessons sink into my brain the best.

Light again on courage, feeling the rocks shaking from fear beneath my feet, I could see the end of the trail. We had only a hundred straight-up feet left to the summit of the peak when my phone rang, in an area where cell phone coverage didn't exist. No one was on the other end, and to this day I believe God was letting me know it was okay to sit this one out. The view where I stopped was spectacular, simply breathtaking and soul fueling. That experience remains one of my favorite reflections of my bravery! I could easily have beat myself up for not making those last few steps, but instead I realized I had conquered my fear even though I never reached the summit. I had more time to just sit there and take it all in, reflecting on how far I had come.

COMMITTING TO COURAGE

When I decided to step into my brave, I went all in. I wish I could insert a video of my first ziplining experience, if for no other reason than for you to hear the beautiful sound of my children's laughter. So imagine me, if you will, white knuckled, reverse bear hugging a tree with my legs trembling on a see-through platform. The beat of my racing heart quickly overshadowed by the sound of two giggling girls. I didn't know whether to laugh with them or cry! What I did know was that I did not want to miss out on a single experience with them, so I plowed through those emotions. I grabbed ahold of my consciousness and reassured myself that the odds were in my favor and that this was *not* life threatening. However, if I were to die, I told myself, I would make quite the big splash entrance into heaven, having fun along the way!

Mystical things happen when we invite faith to the party. Suddenly my anxieties disappeared. Something took over. To my surprise, I let go of the handles, leaned back, and kicked my feet up into the air, placing my body upside down so my eyes could soak it all in as if I had never been afraid. I might even have screamed a big "Whoooo hoooo!"

No matter our struggles we all deserve to experience a beautiful life. There are so many majestic moments awaiting. Trust me when I say you don't want to miss out on one single sensation when you find that right person. The road to finding them can be pretty painful, but I realized the importance of feeling the pain in order to heal and let love in.

Going through a divorce has been the hardest, yet bravest, most peaceful, and most stressful period of my life. A mouthful, I know, but that's the closest I can come to describing it. I learned what I deserve in life and realized the crucial role I play in the outcome. By no means do I advocate for divorce as a quick fix. In fact, I pray that if you are struggling in relationships, you find the "Way." I do, however, encourage you to fight to keep your soul alive, whatever that entails.

LEARNING TO THRIVE

One of the things I instilled in my children is "You must love yourself before you can love anyone else." The Covid-19 quarantine could not have come at a more opportune time in my life, because I had pretty much given up on dating and love. It really tested my initial belief that I would "rather live alone than live like this." Not only did it give me solitude time to check myself, but it made me realize that I had no problem living alone. I did not leave my house for necessities or social interaction for about three months — to the point that my neighbors and children were getting worried.

Honestly, I did not even turn my TV on, yet I never felt alone. I danced in the kitchen, watched my flowers grow, enjoyed candlelight dinners, drank great bottles of wine by myself, learned to Hula-Hoop, cooked via Zoom with my girls, and had beautiful, yummy brunches on my patio while attending online church. It gave me time to reflect on what was really important in my life and what wasn't. It gave me time to heal and reminded me once again how tough I really am.

Putting myself through college, working three jobs at one point to do so, surviving a divorce, and years of off-and-on counseling have taught me that I can make it through just about anything.

The wind might get knocked out of my sails, but an "oxygen tank" is always within reach. What I came to realize is that finding courage in my personal relationships should be replicated in my professional life. The same rules apply. Respect is respect, period, no matter what your job title is. After my divorce I learned that I had zero tolerance for disrespect. The lioness in me had awoken, and my tribe had no room for those who chose to throw poison at my soul or tried to chain me. I had freed myself.

CREATING A NEW NORMAL

Being brave had become a way of life without my even realizing it.

I was at a conference a while back when a previous coworker came up to me and said, "How did you have the balls to do that?"

My initial thought was *What a great line for my chapter in Step into Your Brave*. Then I was like, "Balls to do what?"

My colleague was referring to how everyone in the company had signed the new non-compete agreement with the exception of two people, one of whom had been me. I had refused to sign it after sixteen years of loyal service to the company for which I had brought in multimillions in profits over the years and gone on many sales incentive trips.

I don't know if it was the fact that I was a single mom, about to send two girls off to college and without another job lined up, or the passion and courage she heard during a conversation the entire corporate office listened to when a "friend" called, hoping to persuade me to sign the contract, and put me on speakerphone without my knowing. You never know when you will impact others or who is listening. I wish I could recall exactly what I said that day, but I do know I was brutally honest about how I felt and why I could no longer work for that company. The culture had changed, and our beliefs no longer aligned. My colleague told me that watching me stand strong for what I believed in without fear and with such conviction "changed her life."

It was easy for me to not sign the agreement. The company had lost their focus. No longer was their priority taking care of the customers — or their reps, for that matter. I knew no matter what, I was going to survive. After all, I had the will.

During those sixteen years I made lifetime friendships and met some pretty amazing people who helped mold me into the successful salesperson I am today. I was blessed in my last few years to have a "boss" I worked with about as well as oil and water. You heard me right, I said blessed. He taught me so much about people and leadership styles and gave me reasons to rightfully defend myself, which helped push me into finding my voice and standing up for my professional self. I believe we could have been a great team had he combined the efforts of our unique talents to conquer the competitor, rather than spending energy dismantling our team's drive. Talk about a bubble buster . . .

Gather Your Courage

"Your sales are down," he said. "You have the bull's-eye on your forehead for better or worse, like it or not. That's the way the cookie crumbles. They look for red! It doesn't matter what you did last year, it doesn't matter what you did five years ago. Nobody cares about that."

That is how he justified putting me on a performance plan after I'd been awarded Rep of the Year the previous year, a year in which I had closed the largest sale in the company's history. That was not the first time he had put me on the chopping block without any warning, but I defended it just the same — with facts. The fact this time was that I still had the highest capital sales in the company, but when you looked at growth dollars, which was a comparison with last year's sales dollars, I was at the bottom of the list. In other words, I was selling more capital than anyone else in the company, but I was not beating my own sales dollars from the previous year.

Eventually he wore me down and I signed the performance improvement plan. What was a blindsided, single mom without a backup plan to do? I needed the income to provide for myself and my girls.

The writing was on the wall.

Looking at the non-compete and the path this company was headed down, a direction I did not want to travel, I was not going to let myself spiral down with them. It was no secret; the whole industry knew it. Their focus on taking care of the customer had been lost, and the sales strategy had drastically changed. There was no way I was going to modify my standards just to try to beat myself! Despite the seemingly impossible performance plan my boss put me on, a plan that he was encouraged to lighten a little but didn't, I stoically dodged the bullet and the bounty he had put on my forehead. It wasn't the non-compete that ended that career, it was the disrespect with which I had been treated many years prior.

The ultimatum was either sign the non-compete or be fired, so I quit. Without another job lined up. I wasn't going to allow myself to be trapped in an unhealthy environment.

REDEFINING THE GOLDEN RULE

When I was a kid, my mom always told me to treat people the way I want to be treated. I wish I had also picked up on the fact that I have a say in how I allow others to treat me. I've learned I don't have to give passes to those who hurt me and that it's okay to set boundaries. Learning to limit my circle has created a lot of peace in my life and shown me the power and control I have over my happiness — and over my life, for that matter.

Having the bravery to walk away from that job was so liberating. It has led me to the coolest life altering job on the planet, working with some of the most compassionate people and loving coworkers. We bring innovative products to clinics and communities and help paralyzed individuals walk again. Nothing is more rewarding than seeing the smiles of everyone in the room when we help give them freedom from their chairs. Talk about stepping into your brave — check out #WalkinWithWill to see some of these inspiring, tear-jerking moments as people overcome major obstacles.

It's an amazing feeling when all areas of your life fall into place. I can't thank my mom enough for guiding me to desire a better life at work, at home, and everywhere, for that matter. I would be lying if I didn't say I got my strength from her. My mom has always been my rock. If anyone exudes strength, it's her. I am incredibly blessed to have her as my mother. If there is one thing that she passed down to me, it was her pain tolerance and her fun-loving ways. The women in my family were true warriors. Although their voices may have been silenced, their strength never stopped shining. Watching my mom push through years of pain, hiding all that she was enduring, inspired me to be strong. Her smile stayed big, and her love never wavered. One thing she did not do tough was love. She showed me what unconditional love was and always encouraged me to push myself. If anyone gets credit for helping me step out of the "normal" and into my brave toward happiness, it's her.

I had that same intention for my girls. My failing marriage was not the example I wanted them to view as "normal". I wanted them to have a better relationship, just like my mom had wished for me, with someone who truly loved and respected them. I owed it to them. After all, they are the one thing that kept me alive all those years — they were the oxygen to my broken heart, and the pulse to every beat.

THRIVING ON THE OTHER SIDE

Proof to me that I am right where I belong was evident in a conversation I had with my daughter. She said, "Mom, I feel like you don't share your troubles with me anymore."

It was really refreshing to think about her comment and be able to reply, "That's because I don't really have any. When you surround yourself with the right people and the right environment, life really is *easy!*" And *fun!*

Speaking of easy and fun, this brings us to my newfound love -- a man who no doubt was sent from heaven, one who has restored my belief that love is every bit of 1 Corinthians 13 and more. He speaks in love, and exudes respect. He never belittles me and always encourages me. He protects me to the nth degree and would put his life in danger to save mine, something he has proven many times. I've even tested his anger when I backed my car into the edge of his new garage. That led to my checking his patience as he taught me how to back my car up like a boss.

Of course we have our disagreements and bad days, and struggle some with communication. The difference is that we both use words spoken out of love and provide a safe haven for communication and vulnerability. We fight fair and aren't afraid to own our mistakes and say "I'm sorry." Our disagreements have made our relationship stronger and brought us closer together.

Not to mention he has even helped alleviate my fear of heights. During a trip to Hawaii, he booked a *doors-off* helicopter tour. Oddly, I never felt scared; I can only guess it was because he was by my side. This wonderful, extremely handsome man has somehow effortlessly calmed my fears and made me a better person. I even caught myself thinking as the helicopter tilted to the side, leaning into the edge of a cliff, *At least if I die today, I will die happy!*

I can't get enough of him. I no longer dance in the kitchen alone; he is the first to move the couch and turn up the music. I have experienced what candlelight and rose petals lead to and what it is like for someone to truly put me first. I go to bed laughing and wake up laughing, and sometimes even wake myself up laughing. He believes in me and encourages me and never makes fun of the things I love. Rather, he wants to join in the experience with a "Let's do it" attitude. He makes things I have dreamed of an even better reality. Who would have thought learning to play the drums and congas together could be so much fun?!

He calls himself my Sherpa, because he likes to carry my bags. Not only does he carry my bags, but together we unpack the baggage we have brought into our relationship. Together we remove our dirty laundry, wash it, and repack the empty luggage so we can spontaneously head off to a new unforgettable adventure together. When you come to experience that the best part of a vacation is not the scenery but the person you are with, you know you are in the right place. No eggshells under our feet; there's just sand between our toes!

Love, although not perfect, really can be easy.

I am grateful my parents are still here to see my glowing smile, hear my continuous laughter, and witness the joys that he has brought to my life. When we are together, our love radiates outward. I know it has rubbed off on others and has even softened my dad, turning him into a hugger.

Speaking of my father, fortunately I had the beauty of watching my macho dad transform into a softy right before my eyes when my mom had a major brain aneurysm. I must have heard him say a thousand times as I drove him to the hospital, "I hope she is still there. She does everything!" Luckily she told God she wasn't ninety-two yet and wasn't ready to go. God listened and let her stay here on this earth a little longer.

Gentle love was modeled back to my parents through numerous relationships, and they embraced it. They're like a couple of teenagers dating again, and it is a beautiful transformation to see.

They are so blessed to have had these extra years to live out their second chance at love. A love no longer about control and power or "man of the house" mentality, but more of a partner-in-crime, not taking each other for granted, type of love. My dad refers to "going on dates" and showed his gentle side when caring for my mom during her recovery. I'm not the only one whose chains have been broken and who has been set free.

CHOOSING LOVE

After my divorce, I remember playing a game we called "Would you rather . . ." in which you offered two options for the others to choose from. Someone once asked this, and it has stuck in my mind:

"Would you rather live in a small house with a man who loves you or in a big house with a man who doesn't?"

We all chose love.

I pray big that whether the little humans I created end up in a big house or a little one, their hearts will not question love, their homes will overflow with it the way God intended, and they'll never be afraid to wear their badge of bravery and fight for it all. Everyone deserves a love like this, one filled with peace and joy.

Had I let fear take the lead, who knows how this all would have played out. But fear didn't win, I did!

LIFE IS BEAUTIFUL

Life beyond your brave is beautiful. Don't give fear more strength than it deserves. If you do, you will miss out on so many great opportunities and incredible experiences. Whatever it is you may be facing, I hope the next time fear looks you in the eyes, you laugh, and say, "Not today!" Commit—step into your brave, kick your feet up in the air, tilt your head back laughing, and enjoy the ride. Soak up every moment. May the best part of your journey be the people you are with, not the places you go.

I am grateful for those who have hurt and challenged me, because without those pains I would not truly appreciate the beauty of my present. I also love more deeply because of those who have shown me an agape kind of love. All of which has led me here.

This is the life I want my girls to know, with a love they can't live without.

I'm not sure what the next chapter holds for me, but I know I am not rushing this one; I can't get enough of today. This is a moment in time like I have never experienced before. I am surrounded by so many loving people, I never want it to end.

Gather Your Courage

ABOUT THE AUTHOR
KRISTI KOEHLER

Kristi Koehler, born with a gypsy soul and a heart to help others, is a traveling physical therapist. With a passion for adventure and a fire for improving people's quality of life, Kristi travels across the country with her robotic buddy "Will" helping paralyzed individuals walk again. The name Will was inspired by something her great-grandmother instilled in her as a child, "Where there is a will, there is a way". Her reward is the smiles of people who have been given independence, mobility and freedom from their wheelchairs.

Kristi discovered her own happiness by learning to be authentic, honest and true to herself. Most importantly, she finds her strength and protects her peace by filling her inner circle with loving family and friends along with a positive work environment.

She hopes that she can inspire others to find their will to search for happiness and freedom from fear.

Follow some of Kristi's beautiful, adventurous moments: #WalkinWithWill

Facebook: Kristi Koehler At ReWalk
Facebook/Instagram: PackLight*LoveHeavy

Chapter 3

FOCUS ON HEALING

Amber Wells

"Healing is a lifelong process"

Distant sounds of roaring motorcycles coming down that dusty Oklahoma road made the walls of the tiny single-wide trailer vibrate. A sense of urgency flowed through my five-year-old body.

"Run!" my uncle Jimbo said. "Get into the cupboard! Hurry! Hurry!"

My tiny heart was beating out of my chest as I climbed between two shelves. All I could think was that my mother was going to take me away from my safe place once again. Terrified, I tried not to breathe, afraid that if I was too loud, she might hear me.

As I lay there tensed up with my eyes locked tight, praying not to be found, I heard Grandmommie's voice in my mind with the words she'd often say to me:

"Put your big girl panties on. It's all going to be okay."

NOT OKAY

My father was in prison, my mother in a biker gang. I was "passed around" to live with different family members for years until I was eight, when Grandmommie stepped in, adopted me, and moved me to Florida.

It was the first time I had felt safe and protected, but before long, rebellion, self-harm, and other destructive behaviors became my way of coping with the trauma of the physical, sexual, and emotional abuse I'd endured in my young life.

Because of her age and her health, Grandmommie was not able to keep up with my extensive counseling needs. Eventually, this led to a new nightmare — being adopted by a family friend, a charming fifty-year-old single man; I'll call him Clay. He was a businessman and father of four. Sounds stable, right? But nothing could be further from the truth.

Under his "care" I was slowly groomed for the sexual abuse that would follow. I had no way out and nowhere to go. I remember thinking this must just be how life was going to be for me.

ULTIMATUM AND ESCAPES

By the time I reached ninth grade, my disruptive, self-loathing behaviors had reached a tipping point. When I was fifteen, Clay gave me an ultimatum: either stop skipping school and apply myself or drop out of school altogether and work with him. I chose the latter. The next day I joined him at his painting company.

We traveled the country painting large retail locations. I quickly moved up the ranks. Turns out, it was something I was really good at. Yet there came a moment when I wanted to leave.

I realized I now had a way to save myself. I could put my big girl panties on and get out of this unhealthy, unstable life.

One night as we were crossing over a beautifully lit bridge into Fort Lauderdale, something happened to me that felt like magic. I was mesmerized by the beauty of the place, seeing all the huge waterfront properties and yachts, and experienced an "aha" moment.

I decided then and there to retire the paintbrush and head to corporate America — the place where I thought all successful people were.

I followed through and got a job working for Coca-Cola right before my eighteenth birthday.

NEW DIRECTION AND OLD WOUNDS

I dug in deep. I knew I wanted something more meaningful, so I had to do things differently.

I began to cut off unhealthy relationships to focus on my healing. But it wasn't easy. By age twenty, I had a newborn (conceived during a one-night stand), and we were living in a new city.

Experiencing failure after failure, I knew something had to change. Giving up was not an option. I knew I needed to make a move and switch directions again . . . a feeling I knew all too well.

I started facing my fears. It was time to confront the need to move back to my birth state of Oklahoma to raise my baby boy.

I listened to my gut feelings. Day by day I was relying on them more to guide me. As my gut would press in, it would create pressure out. I began to know this feeling as a conviction for change. I imagine it's similar to the pressure applied to a lump of coal that can be the catalyst for creating a beautiful diamond.

Much like the dirty lump of unwanted coal, I experienced feelings of rejection, unworthiness, and isolation. I mean, how could I ever be worthy if my own parents didn't feel I was good enough for their love and affection?

Over time I shifted my perspective. Thought by thought, I changed my entire mindset. I woke up to the grace that comes only from God, the type of grace that has to meet fear face-to-face and toe-to-toe.

This grace meant I needed to forgive not only each person who had hurt me throughout my life, but also myself so I could stitch up the wounds and shine like the diamond I was destined to become.

Knowing I had to do this, I started conditioning myself with healthy coping mechanisms. I did deep breathing exercises and stretching, and allowed myself to make space for how I felt. I learned how to really sit back, slow down, and listen to my emotions.

I was the one making the calls now. I was in control. I could do *what* I wanted *when* I wanted. Not out of defiance, but from a sense of accomplishment. I didn't have a GED, much less a college degree, but I was full of pride over my achievements. I had never experienced life in this way. I was hitting my sales goals, winning trips, and high-fiving my manager on Fridays. I learned my love languages and began to see why I loved affirmations so much. It finally felt like I had made it.

With my new perspective I was able to forgive all the people who had hurt me . . . and also forgive myself.

As my heart softened, I gave the forgiveness I so desperately needed to give Grandmommie. I started to understand from a different perspective what led to her not being able to care for me and her ultimate decision to put me up for adoption. I was even able to find forgiveness for Clay.

I started practicing practical disciplines such as journaling, meditating, reading self-help books, going to a therapist, and attending a local church. I began to recognize the traits that propelled me ahead as well as the ones that set me back.

UNEXPECTED COMPLICATIONS

I thought I was on the right track in the healing process, and then BAM! out of the blue, I felt all those annoying fears rising up once again.

This time it was a little different. It manifested itself in my switching jobs every two years and taking on much more difficult roles. The harder the role, the more hours I worked. As my pride set in, the pressure of my constant need for control took over.

When I was working, I didn't have to feel my emotions, so I gravitated toward work over and over again, day in and day out. It allowed me to numb out.

I began feeling convicted about the time I was spending away from my son. In search of a better life for us, I got sidetracked. I needed to get back on course and, most importantly, spend more time with him.

All the aches and pains of my heart were now affecting the one human being I loved more than anything in this world: my son. My trauma had bled onto him.

I vowed I would do every single thing that needed to be done to heal us both. With both of us in therapy, I knew the next step was for me to be more available to him. That prompted me to make the decision to leave corporate America.

CLAIMING A NEW VISION

Though I was stepping forward to live out the vision God had placed on my heart, I was not sure how I would be able to support myself and my son.

I took another leap of faith and decided to use the only trade I'd learned to turn a negative situation into something positive. I decided to start my own painting business as a step toward controlling my destiny.

There were a lot of decisions to be made.

First of all, I had to come up with a name, which is a lot harder than one might think. I knew I wanted to make an impact not only in the industry but for women who'd gone through the same kinds of situations I had but endured even worse outcomes — addiction, incarceration, and losing their children.

As the ideas for names materialized, She Paints the Nation stood out as the clear choice. This company would bring the change I had always desired and be a relatable brand for women.

She meaning "you"
Paints representing the ability for renewal, change, and self-direction
The Nation claiming limitless growth while serving the world

Jesus healed nations . . . and I believe I was placed on this earth to be a light in the darkness.

I forged ahead, picked the paintbrush back up, and got my hands dirty so I could paint my traumas differently. They would no longer define me. Instead, they would create a new path for me. I reminded myself daily that I carried the strength of Jesus — the power of God.

NEW SOLUTIONS AND FAMILIAR PAIN

Even though I was beyond ecstatic about my new business, it stirred so many different emotions that a deep depression started to wash over me. Old traumas resurfaced once again, but this time it was different.

When I noticed the familiar symptoms coming on, I responded more quickly than I had in the past. I joined a local church group to draw closer to God, to find my purpose, and to seek divine direction. I needed to find out exactly why my emotions were so unstable.

Through this process it became clear that my purpose is to empower and encourage women to be the boldest followers of themselves through Christ! I knew all along that this desire was inside of me, but this connected the dots to make it real. It was empowering. I was now on a mission.

I realized that all the pain and suffering I had endured in my life was calling me to speak up and speak out for the ones who need the courage to trust themselves.

I reached out to the local women's transitional programs designed to guide women coming out of incarceration by helping them integrate back into society and work toward getting their children back home with them.

This meant I had to stand in the gap between what was once a lost soul and the beautiful woman standing in front of me desiring change and working desperately to get her children back.

This brought joy to the part of my heart that was in need of repair. I was feeling whole again.

BUMPY ROADS AND FORWARD MOVEMENT

As the years passed, my vision stayed true. Because of the healing work I'd done, She Paints the Nation grew in ways that I had only dreamed about.

But with the growth of the painting business, life once again became uncomfortable and stressful — in both familiar and new ways.

I wanted to run — a trauma response from my five-year-old self.

Going back to that little girl and learning that I could take care of her from the age I am today deepened the realization that I wanted to bring this type of healing and awareness to as many hurting women as possible.

It was time for me to power through and once again put on my big girl panties.

With the goal of creating something that would allow the healing process to go more smoothly for women chasing their dreams, I developed a community tied to Grandmommie's legacy. I call it Big Girl PanTees.

It's a safe place for women looking for a sense of belonging and includes a quarterly empowering subscription box consisting of a pair of big girl panties, a self-reflection journaling prompt card, and all-natural self-care beauty products. (I believe if you look good, you feel good!)

But I didn't stop there.

Next, I started to coach women to find their purpose and chase after their dreams, not be held back by their past.

I'm not sure what happens from here, but I know for sure I'm not done yet.

CONTINUING TO LEARN

Just as my business and charitable work grow, I strive to do the same.

I'm bringing lots of lessons into the future with me, but the learning is far from done. As I continue to make my way, I'll keep reminding myself...
- healing is a lifelong process;
- self-love needs to become nonnegotiable;
- until you can love yourself well, you can't fully love others;
- it's important to create boundaries and stop expecting less than what you are capable of;
- putting on your "big girl panties" doesn't mean ignoring the tough stuff going on. It means tapping into your courage to get to the other side.

Step Into Your Brave

ABOUT THE AUTHOR
AMBER WELLS

Amber Wells is a Choctaw Native American from a small town in Oklahoma. She is an international entrepreneur, founding owner of She Companies, Inc. and a selfcare journaling subscription box called Big Girl Pantees.

Little did Amber know that her tumultuous childhood would be the spark to breaking generational curses. Her personal healing journey has equipped her to help others find the importance of self-healing as a step towards rebuilding their lives.

Amber has a heart to help others, passion for the broken, and the drive to create change. She believes that through community she can empower, encourage, and motivate women to show up as the best versions of themselves.

You can find her communities at www.biggirlpantees.com or sheisnextlevel.com.

Chapter 4

BREAK DOWN THE WALLS

Beth Jones

"Each day gives us a new opportunity to move forward with intention."

As my hypnotherapist counted down "three, two, one," I stepped off a staircase I was descending and onto the most beautiful beach I had ever been to. The scene would be a metaphor for the dichotomies of my life: the two lives I had led to this point, the dividing line between my past and my future, and the healing journey I was about to begin that would help me go from just surviving my life to living it, happy and fulfilled.

Stretched out before me was the magnificence of the ocean, the azure-blue waters meeting the horizon. Waves crashed violently on a rocky crag to one side of the beach, while on the other side gentle waves lapped the water's edge under a warm breeze rustling a calm swaying of the palm trees. Behind me was an enormous, towering, and ominous cliff where the staircase I had descended clung to the side.

"Beth, are you in your safe place?" my therapist asked. "Yes," I replied.

"Let's begin. Why are you here today?" In that instant my life changed forever.

In 2020 and 2021, after a traumatic but eye-opening hypnotherapy session, I went through a transformative period. I am highly adaptable to change, but what I experienced during this time was extreme, even for me. I got promoted at work at the beginning of the Covid-19 pandemic. Twenty months later I moved from Hong Kong to Texas. In the interim, I discovered that I am a victim and survivor of child sexual abuse, date rape, and bullying. I realized that I have lived most of my life behind a wall, without the love and emotional support that I need. I began traveling down a path to heal. I got divorced, my marriage a casualty of my healing. I am learning about love and how to get it.

Although those twenty months hold some of the darkest and most painful times in my life, the healing journey that I am experiencing is exquisite. This is my story.

I lived behind a wall for forty-five years, mostly alone.

I had built my forty-five-year tall, forty-five-year thick wall to protect myself from recurring trauma and emotional neglect, but I was trapped behind it. I needed protection from not only the sexual abuse I had survived, but perhaps more detrimental, the emotional toll of not receiving love and nurturing from the three people in my life who should have been able to protect me and support me emotionally. Those were the three people I most desperately wanted to love me — my parents and my now ex-husband, to whom I was married for nearly thirty years.

I used to describe in my own way the abuses that I have suffered. But I never appreciated them for what they were and never questioned why they had happened to me or how they were affecting me. Child sexual abuse I described as being "touched inappropriately." Date rape I described as "a date gone wrong," and I believed it was my fault. Bullying, which came after the rape, I described as "teasing," and I believed I deserved to be teased because of my inadequacies in satisfying my perpetrator.

I suffer from dissociative amnesia, which I believe is my brain protecting me from painful and traumatic memories. This also means I have almost no memories of much of my life. I always found this odd, but only occasionally questioned why I don't recall personally significant events the way others seem to. My memory is void of even milestone moments I should probably remember. I don't remember my sixteenth birthday. I only vaguely remember my high school graduation. Most of what I remember from my wedding day comes from photos or other memorabilia, but I can't relive being there that day.

In my late twenties and early thirties, I engaged in reckless and dangerous behavior, including periods of heavy drug and alcohol use. Sometimes there was illegal activity around me. The drug use would continue, though much less frequently, into my midforties. (The drugs are gone now.) Alcohol could be a problem today if I let it be.

My husband and I created a busy and often chaotic life. I rarely had time for anything other than the constant demands of my career and being the caretaker for him, pets, flocks of poultry, livestock, and the land that was our working ranch. There was also his chronic trauma, including being injured or recovering from fifteen or sixteen surgeries that he had in the time we were together. We were busyholics. And I think we were co-dependents.

Over time my relationship with my parents and my husband became harder and harder. Eventually I became estranged from my parents, our communications reduced to text messaging. Over the years my relationship with my husband became mostly superficial, with much of our communication about chasing happiness through material things. There was little emotional nurturing between us. It has only been during my healing process that I have seen the relationship for what it became — and seen who I was in the relationship. I gave everything to my husband physically, financially, and emotionally. I gave so much to him that I lost myself.

I was cut off from my family and friends who truly love me. This was self-inflicted but also part of my husband's control over me, though the way his control manifested itself was subtle. He did not like my family or most of my friends, and I repeatedly chose the person I had committed to (him) over the people I needed (them).

I locked most of my emotions in little boxes and buried them inside my wall. I cried often but had no idea why. I would cry watching TV or a movie when a loving relationship between two people was portrayed — parent/child or husband/wife — and often in therapy I would sob uncontrollably, with no explanation to be found. On a rare occasion, I would be provoked to anger and erupt in rage. I knew I had repressed emotion, bricks in my wall, but I didn't understand why.

Behind my wall, I could not define my own emotional needs and asked, but could not answer, what my purpose was. I could see only that my purpose was to get my husband through his life. But I eventually questioned, sadly, "Is that all I am meant to do?"

By the age of fifty, I was safe inside my wall, but I was emotionless, and I felt alone. I had no sustained joy or happiness in my life. I could not open my heart to give or receive love. I didn't know how.

I lived different lives, personally and professionally.

Despite the things that were happening to me as my wall built up, I was excelling professionally. Throughout my career my performance has been rewarded with rapid advancement, money, and titles. I've had leadership roles on major projects and then for a practice group across Asia. Today I am well respected and have a voice that can be used and heard at the highest levels of the organization for which I work.

But I often feel like an impostor. Even now it is difficult for me to admit that I am an internationally recognized senior executive. I just don't see myself that way, and it's as if two people are living in my body: the me inside of me, whom I see, and the me the world sees. Often, I have an out-of-body experience where I look over and see the professional me, but I don't feel like that person.

There is a stark dichotomy between my professional life and what my personal life has been like in the past. About eight years into my career, my performance was being reviewed and lauded by one of my bosses at the CPA firm where I worked. We had my performance review over lunch that day. I heard that my performance was above the firm's expectations and in recognition I was being promoted and would get a nice raise and a generous bonus.

I may have still been high when I received this news. I had not slept in over thirty-six hours by then. I had partied through the previous night on methamphetamine, behavior that was common for me back then. As the sun rose that day, I showered, put on my suit, and became another person.

I lived for fifteen years with a recurring nightmare that I didn't understand.

I began having a nightmare when I was in my midthirties, just after a family member — I'll call her Jolene — revealed that she had been sexually abused by a man in our family whom I'll call Joe. In my nightmare, there was a large home where a big family lived. The downstairs was designed for family time, with a large kitchen that opened into a series of family rooms alongside a long hallway. It was set up for happy times, meant to be warm and comforting.

The upstairs was very different. Upstairs the house felt cold and damp. It was haunted by ghosts and demons, infested with insects and spiders, crawling with snakes. Over the years, as I moved closer to the moment when I was ready to begin healing, the house became scarier, more haunted. The house was dying.

Coincidentally, the day I had the nightmare for the first time was also the day that I got back a memory of being sexually abused as a child, probably just before my sixth birthday. This memory is one of the only memories that I have of my early life. It plays like a movie in my head, vivid in its detail of what happened to me that day. I remember feeling intimidated by the towering man that he was, his enormous hands juxtaposed with my tiny body as they moved over and inside me. I will never forget the smell of his breath and body odor. That man, my abuser, was Joe.

The abuse in our family has been a dark secret for all of my life. It is only as the children of my generation have dealt with our manifestations of survivorship that we have begun to talk about and shed light on our experiences. Only now has the reality of the trauma we have survived begun to be accepted.

I never understood my nightmare, or linked it with my memory of being abused, until June 2020, when I underwent hypnotherapy and my truth began to be revealed to me. More about that later.

I searched for the pathway to healing for a long time.

When I look back over my life, I realize my healing journey began many years ago. I went to therapy off and on over the years that I was building my wall, but I never knew why I was there. I never had a therapist who helped me. It was just couch therapy. Some couches I sat on for months; others I left within the first ten minutes.

I took other significant steps toward healing, like when I separated myself from my parents because our ability to interact civilly had deteriorated so badly. For survivors, it's called a "parentectomy," which I describe as cutting off something that is toxic and could have killed me (emotionally).

I took the biggest step when I moved to Hong Kong in 2016. That's where the crucial first real steps in my healing journey occurred. I now see that the move itself was my escape from the physical manifestation of the chaos my life had become. My feeling of imprisonment with no means of escape from the burden of my life was overwhelming. Moving to Hong Kong was me in flight mode.

In 2019 I went through a therapy modality that allowed me, for the first time, to release and understand an emotional blockage. Somatic Movement Therapy uses the connection between mind and body for healing. The sessions were tough for me at first. I was physically rigid — inside my very tall, thick wall — and the therapy necessitated body movement.

One day I moved in just the right way to bring out a flood of emotion, grief, guilt, and shame for the death of my beloved dog, Steele, who left this world a few days before I moved to Hong Kong. She had been viciously attacked by another dog I had allowed to come and live on our property. My husband and I needed the dog's owner as a live-in caretaker at our property in Colorado so that we could make the move to Hong Kong.

I knew there was a risk that our two dogs would fight, because I had seen them interacting before. But in my desperation to move to Hong Kong, I ignored the warning signs, and Steele paid the ultimate price. I was devastated by her death. I was so ashamed of how and why she died that I could not tell anyone about it until that day in the therapy session when I told my therapist. I had no idea I was carrying so much grief and shame over the events of her death and my responsibility for it, and in some ways that emotion was like a bottlecap holding all the emotion I would ultimately release tight within a bottle.

This was the first time I tasted how freeing the release of emotions from trauma can be. It was euphoric. And I wanted more and more as my healing journey progressed.

Hypnotherapy finally put me on my pathway toward healing.

I underwent hypnotherapy in June 2020, a few months before my fiftieth birthday. A few months before the session, I had taken a new role at work that required me to make deeper connections with people than I felt like I could. I found it very hard to do. So, I went to hypnotherapy to seek help connecting with people to build more authentic relationships. I went in naively, with no idea what I would experience that day.

What I experienced was one of the most terrifying events of my life. I reverted to being a seven- or eight-year-old child in a house I recognized as the house in my recurring nightmare. I am almost certain, because of what happened during hypnotherapy, that I suffered or observed sexual abuse in that house, but my brain is protecting me from those specific memories.

During the session, I was panic-stricken and behaving as a terrified, young child, because Joe was in the house searching for me, to hurt me. I was desperately trying to get out of the house, leaving him inside, and trying to destroy the house with him in it. I fought with the house, but I could not destroy it. All I could manage was to trap Joe inside the house, inside a bubble that levitated just off the ground. I was safe enough, then, which brought my panic under control. I returned to my safe place, the beach, and came out of the hypnosis.

That day was the first time I understood my nightmare. I connected the nightmare to the one clear memory I have of being sexually abused by Joe just before I turned six. The session had been painful and traumatic, and I was in shock. But as painful as that session was, it allowed the fragments of my life to begin coming together to reveal who I am, what I have survived, and why I lived behind a wall.

My healing journey revealed itself to me step-by-step, and my wall is coming down.

Hypnotherapy set me on my pathway where I have done my most meaningful work to heal. I've engaged intentionally with each aspect of my healing, and as I am ready to move on, the next step presents itself to me. The crucial methods that I have been using are trauma therapy, reading, discovering my emotional needs, examining relationships, and learning to give and receive love.

I work intentionally and methodically with my trauma therapist. She is a skilled professional who never puts me in a situation where I am emotionally triggered or accidentally uncover repressed memories. I work with her using a therapy modality called Eye Movement Desensitization and Reprocessing (EMDR), through which I have reprocessed much of what I refer to as my "buckets" of negative emotion — guilt, shame, self-blame, and so on — and the associated negative "I statements" that I told myself, each a brick in the wall that surrounded me.

My trauma therapist also helped me through a frustrating and arduous process to identify my two primary emotional needs for acceptance and unconditional love. The moment I discovered these two needs is the moment I realized I had never been loved as I need to be loved. I was devastated by that realization.

I now have a basic understanding of what can happen to a person who suffers the types of traumas I have, as well as the common manifestations of resulting chronic post-traumatic stress disorder, because I read relevant books. There have been eureka! moments for me as I have discovered that what has happened to me in terms of survival is completely normal for people who have suffered trauma. There are words to go with what I could only describe previously, words like *dissociative amnesia* and *parentectomy*. I now know there are four types of survival — fight, flight, freeze, and fawn — not just the two that I had heard of before, fight or flight. I'm primarily a freeze/fawn combination, so fight or flight had never resonated with me.

Although all the books I read are educational, they also have stories of survival and healing. The more I read, the more I realize that I too can heal, and I don't have to live behind my wall anymore.

As my trauma therapy and learning progressed, eventually my observations about the absence of love in my life turned into my quest to find it. Since then, I have been in another intentional process, this one focused on examining my relationships with family, friends, and colleagues. For each relationship I look at how we each behave, observing what I give oftentimes as much as how the other person gives to me. I learn from each of them, how they give and receive love, and how I can give and receive love too.

Today I'm on a quest to know love.

Though I didn't know it until I began searching, I had already experienced love from two of my dearest and closest friends, the women I first told about what I had experienced in the hypnotherapy session and my subsequent emotional distress. I was really scared to tell them because I didn't understand what was happening to me, but I had to talk about it.

It took a lot of courage and a couple of glasses of wine the night I told them. They were shocked. They had a lot of questions, but their questions were from their hearts, filled with genuine care and concern for me.

One of the women is a former prosecutor and had dealt with child sexual abuse early in her career. She was the first person who said the words *sexual abuse, trauma, and dissociation* to me, the last of which I had to research that night. She was so honest when she told me I needed help. Though she meant professional help, which led me to my trauma therapist, I needed much more than that. I didn't know it then, but what I really needed was acceptance and unconditional love, both of which I have found through my friendship with these two women.

In an ongoing expression of love through our friendship, these two women, along with a few others, have held my anger as I coursed through my divorce, holding it in a way that allowed me to transfer the anger to them, meaning that I did not have to hold it inside myself.

Whenever I would get angry at my husband, I would call them and vent my anger, and then they would get mad with me. For me. And I could let go.

Today I don't harbor any ill will toward my ex-husband, and I hope we can remain friends. All these women helped me to not be traumatized further by the divorce itself, and I don't have bad feelings about my ex-husband festering inside of me, potential bricks to shore up my crumbling wall.

I found acceptance and unconditional love through the founder of TALK Hong Kong, a support group for women/femme survivors of sexual abuse. This woman is a trusted confidant because of our shared experiences. I get acceptance from her and the kind of acceptance that only another survivor could have for me. I admire and am inspired by her courage — her courage to be a leader for change, using her own experience to bring awareness to the awful realities of the prevalence of child sexual abuse and to work to shape law enforcement and judicial policy for both victims and perpetrators. I am fortunate to work alongside her in this important effort. She accepts and values my opinion and what I contribute. I urge her to be courageous as she brings her story into the light to help others like me.

I found acceptance in a place that was most unexpected for me. Unexpected because of the dual life I have led personally and professionally. Very quickly after the hypnotherapy session, I had to tell colleagues at work. I was in shock for about two weeks after the session, then took ten days disconnected from the world to be alone and sit with my emotions.

Thereafter in the early days of working with my trauma therapist, I was on an emotional roller coaster, some days so distraught and in such deep despair that I could not get out of bed. As the new leader of a practice group with over a hundred team members, I could not wake up and just check out for the day, though there were many days when I could not function. So, I had to talk about what was happening to me, as best I could at that point, to ask for their help and understanding.

Most of my colleagues I told in the early days were men. I told my boss, peers who technically reported to me, and our head of human resources in Asia, the only woman at work I told at that time. Each of them was shocked and empathetic and accepted what I had to say without question except to ask how they could help me. I think in those moments they saw me as a vulnerable human being who was in pain and needed their support, in stark contrast to the collected businesswoman, executive, and boss they had seen me as before. I felt more acceptance, and I began to see my own courage, which many of my colleagues tell me they see as I continue to share my story more publicly.

Today I am completely transparent at work and answer questions about myself as honestly as I can. I think it is important for someone like me, an accomplished executive businesswoman, who has survived what I have survived and achieved what I have achieved, to share my personal experiences. I do as much mentoring as I can. I often find myself in the mentee role, though, learning from those I am mentoring as much as they are learning from me. These are truly gratifying relationships for me.

One of the most fun and fulfilling ways in which I am experiencing acceptance and unconditional love is through reclaiming old friendships. I do this often and every chance I get. These friends go back to grade school and college, and the early days of my adulthood. Some are friends my ex-husband and I had as a couple. Over time I had become disconnected from most of them for reasons I am still trying to understand. Today I cannot articulate why I pushed them out of my life other than to say I did not stand up for what I wanted, which was to have them in my life.

The reasons why I pushed them out don't matter. What matters is that I kept them all outside the wall around me. From time to time when one would ask to come in and help me, I would reject the person in an angry and defensive way.

I am lucky that each has welcomed me back with open arms as I have reclaimed them as my friends. I've told each of them my story and how I got behind the wall. I've listened as they have recounted stories about their experience with me, often stories that are painful to hear and most of which I have no memory of. I've apologized for my behavior and for not being a better friend. Every single one of them has accepted me with unconditional love.

I've had the opportunity to deepen my relationship with my sister, so that we care for each other like loving sisters should care for each other. We never had this kind of a relationship until recently. She is eight and half years younger than me, and I left home for college, moving halfway around the world, when she was as many years old. I've always felt that we grew up as two only children. As we got older and lived near each other again, we had not developed a strong foundation for a relationship. We too became estranged when I undertook my parentectomy.

My sister has been a safe place to share my feelings in some of the darkest times I have been through in recent years. She listens to me and sometimes offers advice, but she has no judgment. That we have come back together and had the chance to develop a real relationship is so special to me because we've both grown enough to put the past behind us. It was her own healing process that brought us back together about two years before my hypnotherapy. She displayed great courage in inviting me back into her life when she did, and I am so grateful she did, because she was already there when I really needed her. She frequently tells me she loves me. I know what she means. I know it because I feel love for her, too.

My ability to give and receive love led me to fall in love.

My quest eventually turned to my desire to find love in an intimate relationship with a man. I had reached a pivotal point in my healing journey when three significant breakthroughs were coming together. First, I was finally coming through a long and arduous process — about three months — of dealing with crippling self-worth issues caused by my pain and despair associated with the absence of love in my life. I was no longer feeling unlovable.

Second, my feelings for my parents and my ex-husband were giving way to accepting the fact that their own survivorship is most likely the reason they are unable to love me as I need to be loved. I realized they love me to the extent of their capabilities and that what is missing has nothing to do with me.

Third, I was ready to find a man who would truly love me and meet my emotional needs, which I knew by then. I was terrified of the dating process because of the horror stories I had heard from friends my age who were trying to date. I wondered whether I would be able to recognize actions that demonstrated love and the ability to meet my emotional needs. And I wondered whether the man I was looking for, when I didn't know what he looked like, even existed.

He does exist. During the three months I was dealing with my self-worth issues, I had been following him on social media. I had met him many years earlier, and his posts kept popping up on my social media feeds during those months. One day, I finally had the courage to reach out to him.

I don't know what I was expecting at the time. Just reclaiming an old friendship would have been great, but what happened instead has been crucial to both my healing process and my search to find love. This is the relationship where I have experienced the most acceptance and unconditional love. Where I am trying to reciprocate what I have learned about accepting and loving unconditionally. Where I fell in love.

Very quickly after we reconnected, I had to start telling him my story, about my life of perpetual abuse and the path that I was on to break down the wall that I had built to protect myself. He has happy memories of me from our time together when we were young, but his memories are attached to a name — my birth name — which at the time was difficult for me to associate with. He kept using that name, which caused me pain because it conjured up only bad and often traumatic memories of some of the abuse I have suffered within my family. So I had to tell him why he could not call me by that name.

I knew from the way he responded that day that he might be the man I was looking for. He kept telling me the name was a good family name and that even though every family has people in it who tarnish the name, that does not make the name bad. He was trying to get me to accept my own name. But I could not accept it.

So he took me through a process to give me another name that we use privately between the two of us: my given first name, the middle name of his grandfather (whom he adores), and his last name (which he is proud of). He was kind and understanding as we talked it through but also completely selfless in giving up something to which he had attached fond memories to help me work through my pain. Although it was difficult for him to hear, he accepted everything I told him, and for the first time I felt unconditional love from someone who was becoming my romantic confidant.

This man now knows more about me than any other single person in my life. Everyone has their bits and pieces, some more than others, but he has the most comprehensive knowledge of me because he takes care to know me without judgment. To see me. And he's helping me see myself.

He wants me to see the good and beautiful person that he sees. But my impostor syndrome is fighting back. I struggle to see myself as "good," with my inner critic often yelling at me about the way I interact with others, especially my inadequacies in relationships as a sister, friend, and partner. I am an "uncommon beauty," he tells me, knowing I see myself as someone who is ordinary, at best. Sometimes not beautiful at all.

I can be completely vulnerable with him. I can express all my emotions, good and bad, show my flaws, and admit the bad things I have done in my life, and it is all met with acceptance and unconditional love. He's never trying to change me and never asks me to be different — even as I learn to rein in the way I express anger. Unfortunately for him, he's the one on the receiving end of my learning. He hides from me, literally, when my emotions get too elevated.

It makes me joyous after the fact to see what's happening to me as I continue to heal and as we evolve together. I see my ability to let my emotions go, which I could not do behind my wall, though I realize I need to get some under control. Now I laugh at myself and the ridiculous things I do and say out of anger. There's a "conversation piece" in the office room at our home that I created one day when I was in a fit of rage. Yelling at him, I flung open the door to that room, where he was hiding, and the handle went straight into the Sheetrock behind the door. Now I smile when I see the hole, and I probably won't have it repaired until we move out.

We're not perfect as individuals, and we both still have a lot to learn in our relationship. We both know our reunion, at this time in our lives after thirty years of no contact, is by divine intervention and has been given to us at a time when we need each other. Our connection and how we feel about each other has taken us both by surprise. But it is wonderful to be loved and to be in love.

My healing journey continues, and it may for the rest of my life.

Our conversations about me and my healing are ongoing. Because of his patience, caring, and support I have continued to work toward accepting who I am and accepting those who have hurt me. Today I am in the process of taking two significant steps toward reclaiming myself. The first is that I legally took back my family birth name. I think it's cool for my sister and me to be the Jones sisters again.

The other is that I am reclaiming my relationship with my parents. By showing me so much acceptance and unconditional love, my sister and my romantic confidant, in particular, have helped me move toward finding acceptance, and maybe unconditional love, for them. I have done the hard work to get to where I am today, where I can work to rebuild my relationship with my parents, but it is my sister's and confidant's support at my side as I engage with my parents that is giving me the strength and courage to keep going.

It's only after two years of intense and intentional healing work that I can identify myself as victim, survivor, and someone who is doing the hard work to be free of unhealthy survivorship. I have been a victim of various abuses throughout my life — nothing particularly heinous or vicious, but perpetual, and all depriving me of my emotional well-being and ability to be present in and enjoy my life. I am a survivor of all the abuses I have suffered, and through my healing journey am reclaiming my emotional well-being. I am regaining my ability to have and express emotion, good and bad, but most important, my ability to love and be loved. It is through my capacity to love and be loved that I know it will be possible to be happy and to thrive for the rest of my life.

My healing journey goes on as I walk my path and continue to use the tools that work for me. Each day gives me a new opportunity to move forward with intention.

Step Into Your Brave

ABOUT THE AUTHOR

BETH JONES

Beth is a survivor. For 45 years she lived behind a wall that she built to protect herself from trauma and perpetual abuse. Despite her personal challenges, she has achieved professional success as an internationally recognized executive who advises her clients through crisis and transformation.

One day it came time for Beth to heal and she discovered through her healing journey that she had lost herself behind her wall. Put together and successful on the outside, she was empty and felt unloved on the inside. She tells her story of hope to inspire others to heal and to tell fellow survivors that they can find love.

Beth is looking for opportunities to share her story with survivors or organizations working to build inclusive environments where employees feel that they truly belong. To learn more, vist www.iamscorpiorising.com

Chapter 5

REMOVE YOUR MASK

Kim Mittelstadt

"It's okay not to put everyone's needs in front of your own."

In my time of greatest need, I felt alone and abandoned by those closest to me. The ball was heavy and the chains were thick. I was exhausted, overwhelmed, empty, and scared.

I was born legally blind in one eye, and by age three, my eyes crossed on a regular basis, leaving my parents with no other option than to schedule me for an operation to correct my poor eyesight. My earliest memory is of waking up in a hospital room with my hands tied to my crib to prevent me from rubbing my eyes. My parents had merely stepped into the hallway, but with blurred vision and the curtains closed, a feeling of abandonment swept over me for the first time. I was alone.

My mom would attentively attach a small bow to my eye patch each morning before school, doing her best to make me feel special. No matter how hard she tried, I still felt like an ugly duckling. Kids looked at me like there was something wrong with me — like they were afraid of me. They never thought to include me. I felt invisible inside.

Growing up I became masterful at concealing my true feelings, living behind a myriad of masks. I manifested a safe place in my head that resembled a perfectly square "little black box" draped in a beautiful pink satin ribbon that I would escape to where no one could see me. That is where I would store all my masks. From time to time, when I felt brave enough, I would cautiously step out of my box and show up with my favorite mask: "Kim's got it all together."

When my heart felt threatened or I felt alone or scared, into the box I would go until I had chosen the appropriate mask to protect my feelings.

When I was a young performer, my hair and makeup had to look flawless, my costume had to be pristine, and my performance had to be executed to perfection. Messy or sloppy wasn't an option.

I felt most like myself when I was performing, especially sharing the stage with others so as not to be noticed too much. Parades, on-stage baton twirling and dance performances, cheerleading from age seven all the way through high school, playing volleyball either in the gym or on the sand courts at the beach, singing in the choir — as long as I had others by my side, I didn't feel nervous, thinking all eyes were staring at me.

My favorite baton twirling performance memories are of leading our state championship team down Main Street at Disneyland and twirling fire batons for high school halftime shows. Having learned how to be an event coordinator at age nine, I would work alongside my fellow neighborhood kids, organizing our neighborhood talent shows. We even invited the Santa Barbara *News-Press* to venture out to our little street one year to cover our first Happy Face Parade. Our backyard performances would cost the parents a nickel as they filed in through the garage for front row seating.

Most of my first experiences revealed a new mask. The scared little girl walking into her first day of kindergarten with a patch over her good eye, not being able to see and in an unfamiliar classroom. The first grader who got spanked by a nun in front of the class after coming in late from recess because she retrieved a ball another kid had left behind. The second grader who got her name written on the board for talking because she couldn't see the board to know what the assignment was.

I tried so hard to fit in. I thought if I just pretended that I looked like everyone else and was the perfect student, daughter, and friend, no one would notice that I looked different. The harder I tried to be good, the more I found myself in trouble for speaking out or acting up. All I ever wanted was to be seen and heard and yet not noticed. Reflecting on my younger days now, I realize that simply wasn't possible.

I became increasingly self-conscious, especially when I started to go from that "cute" little misfit to a preteen who matured sooner than most of the girls in my Catholic school.

I was known as the class greeter, friendly with everyone. When a new kid was brought to our classroom, I would be the first to say hello, because I knew what it was like to feel alone. I was always eager to make a new friend, yet cautious, in case I had to mask up.

I badly wanted to be in the top reading groups, because they were the kids who were chosen to read out loud. I wanted to read out loud to prove that I was smart too. Only, I failed. I struggled with comprehension, and my grades reflected my struggle. I knew I was smart and that I could learn stuff too, if only I could understand what I was supposed to be learning.

At age eleven, after rebounding from wearing a patch and glasses, my last-ditch effort to try to fit in was thwarted when I was put in a Milwaukee brace for scoliosis. A Milwaukee brace is a fiberglass body cast that starts below your chin, covers you all the way to your hip bones, and ends just above your thighs. There was no chance of disguising myself, feeling cute, or becoming invisible with that thing on.

This only magnified my feelings of inferiority and low self-esteem. The day I walked into my sixth-grade classroom wearing my brace, I was greeted with silence and completely ignored. Later I learned that the "popular girls" told everyone that I was wearing it for attention.

I heard whispers in the hallways, but pretended not to hear them. The infamous mask "Kim's got it together" would magically appear as I choked back the tears. My heart hurt, but no one would know, because I had a mask for that and a place in my head where I could go to feel safe.

The more my heart strove for perfection, the more obvious my failures became to me. I was desperate to escape from the voices in my head telling me that I was worthless, invisible, irrelevant. What I thought mattered was how others thought I should feel on the outside, not how I felt on the inside.

The little black box felt safe for a while, until it became a prison for my soul, screaming to be noticed. The box seemed to have shrunk to a size just big enough to let me gasp breaths of air to exist. My spirit was gone. I wanted to burst out of the box and scream, "HEY, PEOPLE, I'm right here. Please give me a chance. . . See the real me."

I'll never forget the day. . .

As I sat on the edge of my bed and cried, I knew that I had a choice to make. Right there, right then. After "discussing" my feelings about myself with myself, I came up with a reasonable offer . . . to myself. I stood up, wiped away my tears, and took a deep breath. I realized that although I might not be able to do something at that very moment (nor did I have any idea what that something would be), someday I would figure out a way to help others from ever feeling as invisible and lonely as I did. Over the next several years I experimented with all those masks I had collected during my childhood. I left some along the journey and picked up new ones.

With this goal in the forefront of my mind I graduated from high school to pursue a career in cosmetology and attended the Fashion Academy in Costa Mesa, California. Now I had the tools necessary to help other girls and women feel visible and love and embrace the person staring back at them in the mirror, no matter what anyone else thought.

Having worked on my perfectionist skills most of my life, I became the youngest manager of a popular local salon. I was chosen to train under a world champion hairstylist and competed in hair shows followed by several years of working as a makeup artist and stylist for runway shows, pageants, print, and TV.

And then, that girl became a wife. I married Craig, my high school sweetheart, after dating four years long distance while he attended the United States Air Force Academy in Colorado Springs, Colorado. We immediately moved to our first assignment a thousand miles away from the community in which I had spent my entire life. I was eager to begin my life and pursue my dreams of being a wife and mother and making a difference in the lives of others. I expanded my creative mind in all sorts of directions, inventing new and fresh ways to set myself apart in the image and beauty industry, including coordinating style shows and workshops for military wives in our little community.

I will never forget my first transformational makeover.

The doorbell rang as my "model" appeared at my door the morning of the scheduled event. There she stood with her bright blue eye shadow and long straight hair parted down the middle, looking like she had come right out of the sixties. Once she had a new hairstyle and fresh makeup look, and was sporting a light purple floral dress, we headed over to the event center.

No one recognized her! I found out a few days later that her boss of five years was wondering who his new secretary was. But the story didn't end there. . .

A few months later she found me at a military base function. I hadn't seen her since her makeover debut. She ran up to me and gave me a huge hug, and her eyes filled with tears. "I want you to know, you changed my life," she said.

I replied, "I'm so glad."

Then she told me she had left her husband. My heart started to pound, and all I could think was *What have I done?* I myself was newly wed and a new mom, and I had just broken up a family. But then she went on to tell me that her husband had been abusing her and their kids and that my makeover gave her the strength she needed to walk away. Talk about tears. . . I was speechless. That is *exactly* when I knew — without a doubt — that God had had a plan for me all along.

At each new base to which we were assigned, I would connect for a couple of years and offer my gift to empower women before I had to pack up and relocate — leaving new friends and clients behind.

Because of my plethora of masks, I was able to hide my sadness and feelings of loss as we moved around the country.

And then that wife became a mom to, eventually, six children.

Days turned into weeks and weeks turned into years, and life continued to evolve. As much as I tried to keep my entrepreneurial spirit alive, being a military spouse with a husband deployed up to 220 days a year for three years, managing four kids under the age of five (including a set of twins), and feeling the need to show up like I had it all together became a full-time job.

I put my quest to get to know myself aside. Little by little, my personal goals and dreams began to fade, and my life became about everyone else. Folding clothes didn't feel like a chore, because I got to sit down for however brief a moment, and going grocery shopping alone was a chance to breathe and spend time with myself.

I had no other option but to hold our family together, feeling completely alone in yet another unfamiliar small town, while my husband was deployed. I couldn't even find the strength to ask for help. One snowy winter morning while all the other husbands were helping shovel each other's driveways, I noticed I was left shoveling my own. One of the civilian wives actually told me, "You chose this life!"

Another mom decided our kids could no longer play together and that we couldn't be friends because we were six months from getting new orders and, she said, it was too hard for her to have to say goodbye.

Memories flooded back into my head, and I felt the sense of worthlessness, rejection, and loneliness in every fiber of my body. I was too exhausted to recognize the strengths and qualities I had developed over the years. I've got this, I told myself as I stuffed myself deeper inside my heart. I slowly forgot who I had been before I became the person the world told me to be.

Out of sheer exhaustion, old feelings began to disrupt my mind. My favorite mask emerged as my weary body slowly climbed into my old familiar box, now battered and worn, leaving the lid slightly ajar. I had responsibilities. I felt like I was both living in slow motion and spinning out of control.

We had a plan, a dream, and we were making it happen.

The military separation papers were already submitted. Civilian life was only one week away. Training with the airlines was going to start the following week, and I would finally have my husband back.

September 11, 2001. On that day, the world stopped turning, and life came to a screeching halt. Military bases went into lockdown, and airplanes were either diverted or grounded, with all eyes glued to the TV.

In an instant our life went from executing our plan to paralysis. What did all this mean? The rug was pulled out from under us. We now had six kids, a house payment, and no job.

Little did I know that my life, just as many others', would be impacted in a split second — forever. The long-distance relationship, the deployments, had been mere training wheels to prepare me for what the future would soon reveal.

And then Craig was gone. He was sent on a one-year tour in a remote location to save our country's way of life, and I was left behind to save our six kids, ages two to fourteen, alone. I was alone again. My kids became my life. While they attended four different schools, I became chef; chauffeur to soccer, volleyball, football, and gymnastics; housekeeper; tutor; mentor; therapist; personal shopper; mom; and dad. I would roll into bed at night and out in the morning to do it all over again. My body was tired. The stress I carried locked my jaw for three solid weeks, and my back was in constant pain, carrying the weight of the world.

Then one night when all I felt was pure exhaustion, mentally and physically, despair overcame me. Journal entry 2002: *This evening I thought how death is complete; finished; the end . . . and how we spend our lives working so hard for something and then it's over . . .* My cup was empty.

In that instant, I understood the depths of exhaustion and the desperate need for a pause, if only for a brief moment. I reflected on thirty-six years of life experiences and realized it all had a purpose, and that the time had come to step out of the shadows and into my life as the main character and not just as a manager or director or in a supporting role.

Instead of trusting everything and listening to the shoulds and ought-tos around me, I began to trust and understand myself as a whole human. I started listening to my inner voice, my inner knowing, and no longer allowed others' opinions to make me question my own judgment.

In my quiet time, when the kids were sleeping or studying, I read and listened to my intuition speak to me. I listened, I journaled, I asked questions and waited for the answers. I was exhausted, but I was also reawakened to possibilities, to a new friend to trust: me.

My mind became stronger and my masks became part of the past. All but one — the one I spent years refining, my go-to mask, "Kim has it all together." I couldn't seem to let that one go.

As I cautiously stepped out of the shadows, I moved my image consulting agency to a location outside my home. Craig was a year from retirement, and the kids were all in school. It was my time now, time to excavate my buried dreams. Then life threw us yet another curveball.

I was training students from out of town in airbrush makeup techniques when I received a call that my husband's artery had blown and I was to meet his ambulance at the hospital. After his yearlong remote tour, his immune system was shot. Multiple bouts of strep throat had led to either pneumonia or bronchitis, and he had been advised to get his tonsils removed.

I was terrified as I sat in the dimly lit waiting room, alone, in the middle of the night, waiting for the surgeon, someone, anyone, to let me know he would survive . . . My world was shaken, and I couldn't get the look of desperation in Craig's eyes out of my mind as he lay weak and frail in the trauma room, waiting for the surgeon to arrive. After three operations and two blood transfusions, he was released into my care. Some nights I would lie awake and stare at the rhythm in his neck, making sure his heart was beating. After ninety-three days of recovery, he had regained his strength and was able to return to flying.

We had just built a beautiful home in the Texas Hill Country three years earlier, only to have to sell it when PTSD set in from this near-death experience. We needed to move closer to the city, where medical services (and a grocery store) were minutes instead of hours away.

After some time, I was back in my groove, updating my skills as an artist and dreaming and scheming of new and creative ways to relaunch myself and my business. I opened a makeup academy, where I trained makeup artists in new modalities to expand their skills. I also opened my own custom-blend makeup bar where women flew in from all over the country to either train in one of my makeup certification programs or receive a complete transformational makeover.

Our teen self-esteem classes were gaining traction, and life was flowing. I really felt, even without a mask, like I had it all together, I really did.

Until I didn't . . . and impostor syndrome stepped in.

How could I, Kim, have the answers? Who was I to know what was right? My family was my life. My kids and their well-being were always my top priority. No one could love them more than their mom. I was supposed to protect them.

The ball was heavy and the chains were thick.

As I reflect on the sixteen years that we raised teenagers in our home (including four at one time), 24/7, 365, I am grateful that my own adversities gave me the strength and resilience to navigate their various challenges.

Their struggles became my struggles, my heart intertwined with their pain, desperately wanting to take their suffering away. If only I could stand in their place and take their anguish from them.

At times we were met with immense struggles that I, to this day, have no idea how we all survived: bullying that led to despair, resulting in multiple hospital stays on suicide watch; sexual abuse; self-harm; substance abuse; grooming by a pedophile; and mental health issues, just to name a few.

Once I cleared the thoughts in my head and silenced the critics I had allowed to take up space and govern my mind when I was exhausted or overwhelmed, I realized that if I wanted to survive this *and* give my kids useful tools to support themselves through the chapters of their life, I needed to stand up tall and step out of that little black box once and for all. It was time to put down the mask "Kim has it all together" and look at the imperfect person in the mirror with gratitude and grace.

With every challenge, our family learned what it meant to communicate, understand, and accept each other as unique individuals, and we worked together toward new solutions.

The Pandemic of 2020

As I was going through an old file cabinet a few years ago, I discovered a file filled with notes and articles I had written. When I retrieved the folder to reminisce, an old piece of notebook paper caught my eye.

And there it was, a handwritten list of goals from fifteen years earlier I laughed inside as I read the one goal that stood out to me the most: "virtualize your business." I was reminded of the promise I had made to my high school computer teacher almost forty years ago. "I promise I will never touch a computer again if you will just give me a passing grade," I told him as I struggled to understand, let alone figure out how to write, a DOS program.

Covid-19 changed everything. The world quite literally shut down. Eight weeks after our grand opening, we were forced to close the doors to the custom-blend makeup bar we had just opened in our local mall.

"Virtualize your business" kept creeping into my mind. Businesses all over the world were converting to virtual to survive. But I had made a promise to my teacher, and talk about a block! I had so much to catch up on related to technology. I had been depending on my kids and their knowledge for far too long, and if I was ever going to virtualize my business, it was time I became a techie. After shaking off the heaviness of that promise, I took a monumental step into the unknown and began to learn new tools and techniques to develop my technical skills.

While grounded an entire year in our homes as the world tried to figure out how to move forward through sickness and deaths, the meaning of life became clearer to me than ever before.

I've spent an entire lifetime searching for answers, hiding my imperfections, when all along, the answers have been revealing themselves to me.

Every obstacle, disappointment, bad choice, and promise has been transformed into a priceless lesson. My life has unfolded uniquely and beautifully *for* me, not *to* me.

It was time for that carefree, life-loving, happy little girl who still lived inside of me, who so desperately wanted to be seen and heard all those years ago, to grow up and step out of the shadows and into her spotlight and take the leading role in her life.

A few years ago my youngest daughter presented me with a book of favorite "Mom quotes" that all the kids valued and applied to their lives over the years. Oh, my heart . . .

"Wherever you are, be there." *We all get so caught up in the little things around us that we forget to enjoy the present. Thank you, Mom, for teaching me to love the here and now and to hold to the good times as long as they are here.*

"Do *your* why or why not, not someone else's." *Growing up it's easy to lose yourself while trying to figure out who you truly are. Thank you, Mom, for showing me that I am a perfectly unique young lady.*

"Meet people where they are." *During life we meet so many new people who have different priorities. Thank you, Mom,* for teaching me to meet everyone where they are instead of taking it to heart when I feel like I was the only one trying.

"Stay in your lane." Never let someone else's journey get in the way of your own. Thank you, Mom, for teaching me not to take others' journeys personally and to continue to focus on my own goals.

"Stay in your bubble." This one is very important to me. This taught me how to set healthy boundaries for myself. Without this I wouldn't be as independent and understanding of others. This quote is a nice way of learning personal space.

"You don't have to be friends with everyone, but you have to be friendly." This helped me understand the differences between people. You may not click with everyone you meet, but you should always be kind. Thank you, Mom, for teaching me to be a kind-hearted person.

"All you can do is all you can do." No matter what, there is only so much that can be done, so why stress? Thank you, Mom, for making me understand that stressing isn't going to help the outcome.

As I teared up in the audience, listening to my son refer to my most infamous quote of all, "Wherever you are, be there," as he shared it throughout his entire valedictorian speech from medical school, I realized that I *had* kept my promise to my teenage self all those years ago. I had been making a difference all along.

I saw the world with new eyes and understood that imperfection was more perfect than perfection. I was reminded once again that living by others' expectations no longer served me. I was good enough. *I am good enough.*

My weaknesses became my strengths, and my imperfections became the perfect teacher. I know that while I was living in the busyness of life and exhausted, I never could have taken the time to process how I could do things differently. I was existing, not living.

If I had known what I know now, I think the journey might not have felt so heavy. Through all the trials, experiences, and knowledge that I've gained over the years, I've learned how to be still and listen to my heart. My most difficult task, to this day, is learning that it's okay not to put everyone's needs in front of my own. But I am a work in progress, and that's okay.

My trials and life experiences are what made me who I am today. I'm truly grateful. I learned so many lessons amidst the chaos.

Life will unfold in its own beautiful, magical way, and it brings me great joy to help other women and teens discover how they can step into their own brave.

Remove Your Mask

ABOUT THE AUTHOR

KIM MITTELSTADT

As a teen, Kim struggled with body issues, being self conscious became her norm. It wasn't about the clothes she wore but the body she was wearing them on. This set the stage for her motivation to fulfill a promise to her childhood self - that she never wanted anyone to feel as alone and self-conscious as she did. The sadness and frustration was further validated in adulthood when she recognized other moms shared the exact same struggle.

As a retired military wife and mom of 6 now-adult children, Kim knows what it means to play a supporting role in everyone else's life. Her experiences have culminated into her life and style coaching practice helping moms develop a positive body image, (re)discover their passion and joy to become the ultimate example for their daughters.

Head-to-soul beauty is an inside job. Kim believes when you learn to truly love yourself and let go of others expectations you hold the blueprints to live a happy, healthy life.

If you're ready to step out of the shadows and into your spotlight, connect with Kim at www.midlifestyling.com

Chapter 6

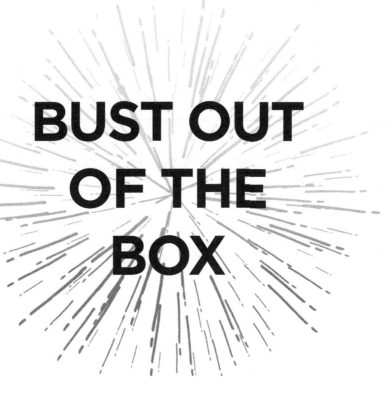

BUST OUT OF THE BOX

Katharina Stuerzl

"New awareness feels like freedom and inner peace."

Growing up in Germany, I learned the best manners, the appropriate etiquette. I knew how to behave so everyone would view this tall, blond girl as elegant and poised. Pretty eyes, bright smile — always polite, joyful, and kind.

Throughout my teenage years, reality on the inside often felt different from *fine*.

After my parents' divorce, food became my shelter, my shape got out of control, and my sense of worthiness depended on validation from others. I *desperately* tried to fit in. Not just into my jeans. Transitioning into adulthood became about losing the weight of expectations, cultural programming, and being perfect.

EXPECTATION, JUDGMENT, AND PAIN

Growing up, everything had to fit into the box that I learned was the *right* one. There wasn't much space for any gray areas.

During our German *Abendbrot* (dinner) each evening, my brother and I shared our experiences from our day. We categorized them as good or bad. We criticized our friends for how they had misbehaved, and talked about how we were right. We judged, and we labeled things and people with expressions we had available in our box. But I remember my intuition whispering in my ear, *What if there is a different perspective for that? What if we are wrong and they are right? What if both opinions can coexist? What would happen if I decided to break the cycle and seek open conversation?*

Whenever I took all the bravery I had inside me and *did* speak up, I got shut down with harsh disagreement. "Oh come on, Katha, do you always have to understand everyone and everything?!"

And that was it. At school, teachers would always encourage us, "Speak up, don't worry, there is no right or wrong, and there are no silly questions." Yeah, sure, we all know *those* phrases. They are usually followed by a pair of rolling eyes, a look as if you are an alien, or, yep, harsh disagreement.

Guess what I decided? That it was much safer in my box. I did not speak up anymore. Not at school, not at the dinner table at home — especially when I had a different perspective to offer.

My heart got broken once when I confronted someone I loved. Like it was yesterday, I remember begging my dad to admit he had lied, just so I could forgive and trust him again. Just so I would not lose him through my parents' divorce.

Come on, Dad, at least admit that you just lied to my face. I heard the woman's voice on the other end of your phone — it wasn't your boss. He confirmed that the two of you did not have a call.

Well, my dad did not confess. I saw only one way out: separation. I made the choice to not see him again, because I felt disturbed. I felt I could not trust him anymore.

Back then I had no clue about the scar it would leave on my soul. Looking back today, I often wonder how that experience is related to my not speaking up in relationships, even though I felt the nudge to do so.

I remember seeing him leaving, knowing that *that was it*, and hear my mum's voice in the back of my head: *Honey, remember, God gave us language to hide our true emotions and opinions, so that you can respond in a way that serves you better.*

Dang it, maybe she was right about that after all. Maybe I would not have lost him if I had put a smile on my face and processed the pain with my mum afterward.

Proper dinner etiquette, friendships, body image, external appearances, and the image of a harmonious family were some of the social norms my life revolved around. My sense of belonging? Totally dependent on whether someone else approved of me.

CONFLICTS, DISAGREEMENT, AND SHAME

Conflicts were hidden behind closed doors. God forbid the fights escalated and *our neighbors could hear us arguing!*

"Shh, Katharina, they can hear every single word! What will they think?" I hear my grandma's voice like it was yesterday. *Well, they talk about us anyway, right?* I heard my intuition whisper again. *Maybe we can speak with each other instead of yelling at each other just to get the emotions out.*

I don't know about you, but our arguments never ended in closure. To be honest, most of the time we did not even know what the actual argument was about.

The pattern was always the same: layers of frustration would build up, someone would take something personally (so typical of the German culture!), and then *boom!* sounds of hysteria, anger, and forceful speech would fill the rooms of our generally loving and warm home.

I did not really learn what it meant to let go of being right. Being vulnerable and admitting mistakes was viewed as weak and shameful. So yeah, when my dad did not admit to his mistakes, I saw only one way out. Black and white, right or wrong, remember?

Have you ever heard of ghosting? Disappearing from someone's radar? It's something I have done a lot with my friends. Find a couple of character traits that didn't fit the ideal image of friendship? Yep, you've guessed it, that was it. If only I had listened to the nudge my intuition whispered in moments like that: *But what if there is more than just right or wrong? What if the middle, the paradox, offers an opportunity?*

I'm not sure if you can relate, but breaking up girlships (friendships with girls) feels just as awful as breaking up with your first high school sweetheart.

What I have done did not demonstrate an elegant and poised demeanor by any means. It was easy, but not genuine, not joyful, and not kind. Nor did I honor who I wanted to be in this world. It wasn't until much later that I came to understand how important it is to honor your authentic self.

You can imagine, with this approach, that I did not have many friendships or connections in my life. This restless and lonely feeling pushed me harder to try to fit in. Remember, one thing I had learned was to behave well, to assimilate. I managed to put a mask on to fit in with the cool kids. I tried to mimic their identity, tried to laugh about jokes they shared, even though I would secretly catch myself thinking, How mean is that? How stupid! That's not funny, that's condescending!

Although it looked like I had tons of friends and was going out every weekend, I often felt the opposite on the inside. I remember those parties like they were yesterday.

I hope they don't discover that I am uncool.
I hope my shirt is not too tight and people can see my belly.
I hope there is enough space on the couch so I can fit too.
I hope I have cool things to say!

Do you remember the scene in Harry Potter where Harry begs the Sorting Hat not to put him into Slytherin? That was me at every party, begging, *Please don't exclude me from your box, please allow me to belong, please just see me.*

In my obsession with trying to fit in, I forced myself to figure out what I could say that others might find interesting or worth a conversation. Just recently I read in Brené Brown's *Atlas of the Heart* that "true belonging doesn't require us to change who we are; it requires us to be who we are." You have no idea how much I wish she had written that twelve years ago.

What I thought was true belonging was me becoming a marionette to those around me. If anything, it pushed me further away from who I truly was and maybe wanted to be. Quite frankly, I had no clue who I wanted to be; I just did not want to feel the pain of being left out, left behind, or, worst case — rejected and ashamed.

Coming home after uncomfortable nights like those, I needed my mum's shelter. I knew she would give me the external validation I was looking for. Well, partially. Although she said I was pretty, smart, and great the way I was, something in particular was not so great about me — something she (and her cultural upbringing) identified as part of the reason I could not fit in or belong. Unfortunately, that tiny little problem was in fact not so tiny; my belly was often referred to as a swimming ring.

As I was shoving my fatty cheese, midnight snack sandwich into my mouth, dripping butter all over the plate, my belly hurt. I knew eventually the physical pain would tune out the emotional pain and I could cry myself to sleep, only to put my mask of perfectionism back on the next morning. As I tried to numb the disappointment and pain of loneliness, my mum looked at me with concern in her eyes and said, "I really want you to lose weight. People are talking about you. They might smile to your face, but they are looking at you with disgust. I see it in their faces."

Ouch, that hurt.

I put the plate down because I could feel my throat tightening, my face heating up, and tears, one by one, rolling down my cheeks.

"If only you would lose a couple of kilos, they would stop talking about you," she said. "They could see how beautiful you are, and would accept you for who you are."

Honestly, I don't even remember if she added the second part of the sentence, but that was what I took away anyway.

Having a sense that my mum came from a place of love and worry that her daughter would be hurt and shamed by others did not erase the statement that my heart and soul remembered: "People are talking about you. They might smile at you, but when they look at you, they talk about you badly."

To be honest, today I am thinking that I had no clue whether they would judge me, but back then, that statement made me judge myself even more. Back then I had no clue that self-judgment would lead to more suffering, which would lead to self-shame and blame. What a vicious cycle, let me tell you. Here's the thing: when others looked at me, I did not give myself even the slightest chance to believe they might think or say something positive about me, whether it was related to my shape or to my intelligence. Her statement triggered in me the belief that people were about to embarrass or shame me. Unless my gut promised me I was safe around someone, I would not open up.

FRIENDSHIP, INTERFERENCE, AND WITHDRAWAL

During my college years, I did have one friendship, with a young woman called Linda. One that my gut trusted from the early stages of our friendship. One I opened up to.

We met at the birthday party of a common friend. We started talking, and she inquired about my interests, what I liked in school, what my hobbies were. She embodied freedom, joy, drive, passion, humor, and action taking. She and I hit it off right away. She drew me in with her wild and free spirit. There was no filter. Understanding each other almost blindly, there was this trust, support, care, light, and joy I had been craving so intensely. She and I just happened — I did not force it, and neither did she.

I think what fascinated me most about her was that she did *her* thing, had a vision for her life, and had dreams, and allowed mine to coexist with hers. If anything, she helped me see a dream, a vision. I think she was the first to ask me, "Kate, what does your gut say?" when I stood at a crossroads.

External voices explained to me that she was not well mannered enough. That she was too bold, too rowdy, too loud.

Through a series of events, in which I looked for evidence that my trusted advisers were right with their evaluation of our friendship, I distanced myself from her. At some point, it felt like a ticking bomb, because I had no clue what to say anymore when she confronted me about why I was pulling away. It was easier for me to escape and to end the friendship with "Look, I don't agree with the behavior of our clique. Therefore I am okay with not having contact anymore."

That was it.

I did not speak about my emotions. I did not truthfully share my vision of true friendship — that I thought we should not talk *about* each other but instead should talk *with* each other.

By not being forthcoming, I did not walk my talk, though. Instead of starting to have honest conversations and allowing one of my friends to disagree and point out the positive sides of our friendships, I pulled away from *all* of them. To overcome the pain, of course, I let others' validation override the contradiction and confusion in my heart and in my gut. My mind and heart were spinning.

I was torn between relying on the guidance of my trusted advisers who had been the stable constant in my life after my parents' divorce, and the joy, freedom, and wholeheartedness of my friendship with Linda. I chose to stay in the safe zone and to rely on others' opinions more than on my inner compass, my gut.

LIFE, LIBERTY, AND THE PURSUIT OF HAPPINESS

On March 26, 2016, I landed at JFK airport in New York in the United States of America. All by myself. With three suitcases, waiting for a driver to take me to my new home in Schuylkill County, Pennsylvania. What critics had called the middle of nothing turned out to be the middle of everything for me: it was the beginning of a journey to myself, to true belonging. The next day was the first day of my internship at a medium-sized manufacturing company. Toward the end of my master's program in North American studies I felt the urge to explore U.S. culture myself. Looking back, I often wonder if I knew that the U.S. culture of freedom would become my safe haven.

The only thing I knew back then was that far away from comfort, the known, and my personal advisers in the form of family members, friends, and professors, I leaned into my curiosity and inner calling of redefining myself.

I remember arriving at the old Victorian bed-and-breakfast, my new home for the following months, carrying my suitcases upstairs to my room, taking a shower to wash away the tiredness, sitting down on my bed, and thinking, *Well, now what?*

Quite a few minutes of stillness went by (you could have heard a feather drop to the floor), and I literally thought to myself that *this* actually felt like a fresh start.

Inside of me, I felt the excitement of redefining who I was. I had nothing to lose. The next nine months were mine to play with and my chance to see what would actually happen if I explored the paradox, the gray zone I had longed to explore all my life.

I grabbed my journal and documented all these new feelings of *excitement, freedom, joy, and fearlessness*. I spent quite a few hours filling the pages of my travel journal with questions:

- Who do I want to be?
- What does *being* me mean? What does it *feel* like?
- How do I show up tomorrow?

After jotting down the answers in my notebook, I got tired and fell asleep, feeling both peaceful and excited.

Something was about to change. I just *knew* it.

I remember pulling into the parking lot of my new workplace the next morning. The yellow building was shabby, the interior with wooden paneling from the 1970s. I thought, *Ooo-eee, not my style, but hey, you are in America — who cares about the interior style, really?!*

If you are curious about how my first day went, you'd better be prepared to be in a space right now where you can laugh out loud.

As I sat in front of my supervisor Bill, a seasoned businessman, very formal and well spoken, he asked me to fill out some paperwork. Once I'd completed several papers, I wanted to staple the pages together. *Nothing wild*, you think. Well, the challenge was that in that moment, at that time, I had *no clue* what the word for stapler was.

Bust Out of the Box

Although I had set the best intentions to "just be me," Bill's presence intimidated me. I didn't want to appear stupid, as if I weren't knowledgeable enough, or was incapable of mastering the English language. My professor's words were in my ears: *Your skills are not good enough for us to write you a letter of recommendation. You won't ever be able to make it in an English-speaking country.* Realizing I was drifting out, almost giving in to the conversation in my head about this past experience, I caught myself: *Focus, Katharina! Come on!*

My eyes slowly moved over the surface of Bill's desk, my heart beating in my chest. I kept looking for the thing whose name I did not know. Finally, I spotted the object I desired so much sitting on the other side of his desk. *The hell with it*, I thought. *Why not just pronounce the German term in English?* Now, let me tell you, with some terms that works, but I learned that with *this one*, it made absolutely no sense at all for Bill! But here I went:

"Bill, could you please hand me the tacker?"

Silence.

I held my breath as his very confused eyes stared at me. He politely repeated what I had asked for, trying to figure out what I could possibly mean.

"The *tacker*," I repeated confidently, this time pointing at it.

He looked at me, looked at the "tacker," looked back and forth a couple of times to make sure he understood correctly, and then started laughing out loud. His joy-filled laughter was contagious! I could not help but chime in and ask, "What? Is something wrong?"

Still laughing, his response was priceless: "Well, originally this thing was called a *stapler*, but from now on, I for sure will call it a *tacker*."

This experience, along with many others that followed on this journey to myself, allowed me to learn how to let go of the need to be perfect and fit into a box of expectations and instead just speak my mind, encounter the world with my open heart, show enthusiasm about the little things in life whenever I feel it, and think, *What is the worst that can happen if I make this step?*

Throughout the internship, I leaned into my curiosity, and learned to listen to my gut and step into my brave a couple of times. One time was to bring my idea to paper and life to complete my master's degree with a study about the Mergers and Acquisitions of the companies I interned for. The internship opportunity turned into a full-time position in human resources that would allow me to make a difference in the people operations in the firm where I saw *so many opportunities*. What was different in my U.S. life from life in Germany? I am not sure; I always say it is a *feeling*. The one thing that felt different for sure was that people were not laughing *at or about* me anymore but lovingly *with* me when

I explained I wanted to be both a gymnast *and* a doughnut-lover.

Was I scared of pushback? Did I hear a no? Of course I did. Plenty of times! But I handled it differently. Instead of hiding in my corner and withdrawing from my vision because of a no, I explored what I could learn from feedback. What was true about my critic's perspective? I think I learned to understand that critics don't necessarily come from a win-lose perspective; sometimes they just can't see what you see. I began to lean into the gray zone and to play with different approaches.

CHOICE, CURIOSITY, AND GROWTH

Even though I made choices that my heart screamed yes to, what I had not let go of was the judgment piece of my cultural upbringing.

I still wanted others to behave in what I considered the "right" ways. I wanted to puzzle-piece them around my vision. By doing so I distanced myself from accepting others' true colors and continued to judge them as right or wrong — which created the feeling of being out of alignment with my "who" again. Following the nudge that I had some more internal work to do, I hired a coach.

In one of our sessions, while preparing for a fierce conversation with my boss, I shared how I felt his demeanor was one of constant conflict and defense and how hard it was to convince him of my project ideas for how to improve our company culture.

After I'd laid out my monologue of how he was at fault and why he needed to respond differently to my pitches, my coach leaned back, looked at me, and said, "Well, that sounds pretty judgy, don't you think?"

Boom. I felt pushed back into my seat and felt my cheeks getting rosy. Had she just called *me* out on being *wrong*?

"What is your intention with the conversation?" she challenged me.

I said, "Well, to voice that we have to put the problem in front of us and both work toward it instead of fighting against each other and getting nowhere." I paused while she held space for me so I could reflect and sit with my emotions.

Then it dawned on me. *Would it make sense that my thoughts have an effect on my demeanor?* "I wonder how I could impact the conversation in a deliberate way, if I saw every interaction with him as an opportunity instead of being afraid of conflict. I guess when I enter our conversation thinking he will disagree anyway, my demeanor probably has an effect on his response, too. Doesn't it?"

"Bingo! You got it," she confirmed with the smile she always has when she's proud of me for making a huge breakthrough. "So, what other choices do you have?"

From then on, I entered every conversation thinking, *What impact do I want to have, and how do I show up in alignment with that?*

I started to make a conscious effort to choose language that was nonjudgmental and curious as often as possible. To own my response to situations and people. To not accuse and assume people's intentions but instead to openly inquire. For example, "Out of curiosity, why do you feel so upset about this meeting?" and "Help me understand what led to your behavior the other day."

I chose to show up with curiosity and compassion toward their perspective. Through that experience I have learned to explore the feelings that arise when something triggers me. When I feel the need to defend myself. "To be honest, when I shared my idea, your first response seemed defeating to me; I wonder if we can have an open conversation about it." Or sometimes, when I feel hurt or heated, I just manage to say, "Can we talk about this on a different day? I feel like I need to step away."

Brooke Castillo from the Life Coach School talks about how emotional pain is the worst of all pains. Not because of the pain itself. But because of the fear of the pain, we don't lean into growth and courage. Once I learned to lean into uncomfortable situations, to hold and survive silence, I began to feel inner peace and strength. It is the pathway to freedom.

Once you understand your triggers, and how we connect present experiences to past moments, you can own them. Even better, they don't hold power over you anymore. You can comprehend them, and why you feel the way you feel, and realize that the past is different from the present.

You have the choice how to respond this time. Today, when I feel nervous or restless, and I want to numb it with food, I pause for a second and ask myself what I truly want right now. It doesn't always go smoothly, but I can tell you I don't have to squeeze into my jeans anymore ☺

In my own coach training program, I had such an experience in our second module. Just to paint the picture: in module one, we all came together as blank pieces of paper, connected in our purpose of becoming coaches to empower others to find their purpose. We did not know much yet, but by the time we came together for our second module, we had learned some skill sets.

Boy oh boy, did I feel the pressure to do.it.right. Even worse, I watched my peer coaches like a hawk, to see if they applied the tools the right way or I had a better idea. And when one of my peer coaches started to criticize people, I thought, *How dare you criticize us? We are here to learn. Stop judging*. Get it? I judged someone else for judging while judging myself. Ha? Yes, exactly.

Our second module catapulted me back into perfectionism and performance mode. . . into having to show that I am good enough to belong to the coaching profession. I let go of the playfulness and purpose-driven feeling from the beginning of our certification program and, once again, leaned into old habits and judged others and myself.

That night, I felt like crap. And I *knew* I had to get to the bottom of it. I grabbed my journal and wrote everything out, exploring what had triggered me and why.

That journaling allowed me to sit with the emotion. To hit the Pause button before going further down the judgment spiral.

Leaning into perfectionism and judging others was not who I wanted to be; if anything, it was the opposite of my purpose and my "who." Why the hell did I do it?

Seconds went by, and I wondered off to try to re-feel the emotion in the moment, when I found flaws in others. I took a deep breath in. And a deep breath out. In. And out. And there it was: the clear sense in my gut that the moment I found a flaw in someone else, I got my validation that I was good enough.

That when I looked on the outside, I did not need to turn inward to take responsibility.

And the reason it felt like crap only minutes afterward and lasted throughout the day? Because it was not sustainable. I still did not feel better about my own actions, my own performance. It is like overeating. It feels great in the moment. But in reality, judging others, numbing the emotional pain with physical pain, only overshadows the truth, which is that perfectionism and judgment does not serve you a bit.

It does not make anyone or anything, and certainly not you, a bit better.

What *does*? you might ask.

Well, let's take a peek at my journal entry from October 30, a brisk, sunny day in Pennsylvania.

Kat! If you want to be comfortable with your coaching skills, you have to be present! You have to play all out. Take responsibility and ownership for your shortcomings. Study more if you are not happy where you are. Learn from your peers instead of judging them! Jesus, Kat, how uncool of you to find pleasure in criticizing others!

I paused, and wrote, *But Jesus, Kat, great job in recognizing it! Sitting with it and owning it! And tomorrow, Girl, go out and play! Be present and cheer your mates on! Be bold! Be joyful and curious!* Teary eyed, I could sense a bright smile on my face. One that felt very real, very authentic. Not just for show.

That night, I consciously chose to check in with myself, my feelings, the signals my body sends in every moment, to explore them, to be present, and to play life full out. To lean into opportunities, to speak my truth and to own both my losses and my wins. To learn from mistakes, and to jump into new adventures.

This new awareness feels like freedom and inner peace. I actually feel powerful. Yes, powerful. In a calm and tranquil way. Understanding that I can read and understand my own emotions, my triggers, that it is okay to sit with them and to consciously choose my response, brings the freedom of relying on myself. Understanding my emotions helps me recognize when I am deflecting (tuning out an emotion by doing something else like overeating). In these moments, when I recognize it, I have control over my actions. I can choose. I can let go of the dependence on external judgment. Choosing my behavior consciously allows me to be in alignment with who I want to be. Authentically and unapologetically.

FULL CIRCLE CONNECTION

Because of Covid-19, I did not travel back to Germany for three years. On March 1, 2022, I landed in Frankfurt. I was nervous. I was shaking inside.

I used a couple of coaching sessions to prepare myself for this trip. Remember, when I left Germany for good in 2019, I did not feel like I could practice self-expression in the country I grew up in. I felt like I could not breathe until I had American soil underneath my feet, and when I left, I knew I would leave family behind who are quite okay with the German lifestyle.

To say I was anxious that my approach to life would collide with how my German family continued to live is the least I can say here.

My mum had decorated the whole floor of the apartment house in excitement about my arrival. Climbing up the steps to my parents' apartment immediately put a smile on my face, and I felt welcomed and loved.

The challenge remained. My parents and I, especially my mum and I, had to reacclimate to each other. I wanted to share my impressions, my feelings, but I also did not want to hurt them when speaking about how I loved my new life, freed from a box, in the United States. While strolling through a farmers' market, my mum and I overheard conversations. Take a guess what I picked up on within seconds. Right: there was so much judgment and so much defensiveness in people's tones. Later that day, my mum was actually the one seeking the conversation around the differences in cultures.

She said she felt that in her world, everyone seems to be out for themselves. *Now, isn't that interesting*, I thought. *No wonder, when everyone puts everyone in a box and judges others as right or wrong. How can you possibly create connectedness?* But I did not say anything. And in that moment of silence, her gaze stopped at my open laptop and she read out loud the quote on the screen:

> *Connection is the energy that exists between people when they feel seen, heard, and valued; when they can give and receive without judgment; and when they derive sustenance and strength from the relationship.*
> —Brené Brown, *The Gifts of Imperfection*

"That's very true," she said, deep in thought.

"Yeah, when you let go of judgment and see the person for who they are, you build a world of connection," I added. She looked at me and smiled. I knew she understood.

And that afternoon, we built tons of connections. We spoke about certain things she taught me as a child and as a teenager that I shared do not serve me anymore. At first, she fell into a defensive tone of voice and explained how that was not how she meant it and that certain pieces of wisdom have served her many times. The feeling of annoyance came up inside me. However, being on the growth journey of meeting people where they are, letting go of being right and wanting people to behave how I expect them to, I chose a different response.

I let her finish and gave her space to share her perspective, and this time our disagreement did not end in an argument.

Instead, we hugged and said, "I love you," and she added, "I'm proud of you for who you became."

Even though certain ideals that my family had don't serve me anymore, my mum still plays one of the most important roles in shaping who I am.

It is because of her that I cherish the little things in life. It is because of her that my heart is grateful and my spirit is joyful, warm, and generous.

Just like people are not right or wrong, neither are cultures. Part of my inner peace and serenity today comes from the fact that I am appreciative of *all* my life experiences, especially the uncomfortable ones. They make us resilient.

I am beyond grateful that my journey to America broadened my horizons and that I learned what it means to have the freedom of choice and to let go of judgment and categorization.

Bust Out of the Box

ABOUT THE AUTHOR

KATHARINA STUERZL

All her life, Katharina tried to fit in. . . into the box society made for her and the story she was telling herself. Moving to the USA from Germany literally catapulted Kat out of that box. Today, she's left fear of judgment and need for outside validation behind.

Taking responsibility for her own thoughts, feelings and actions helps her create the life she desires. She speaks up fiercely in full conference rooms in defense of diverse ideas and perspectives.

As a life and leadership coach and motivational speaker, Kat inspires people to confidently get out of their box. She helps them align what they do with who they are and what they value most. She draws on her experience in HR to energize leaders and challenge them to value the individual in support of the collective.

Outside of her professional passions, you can find Kat outdoors hiking or biking with her husband, at live concerts with her friends, or enjoying a nice cup of cookie-dough ice cream, her all-time favorite!

Connect with Kat through LinkedIn, or visit her website www.leaveyourboxwithkat.com.

Chapter 7

KNOW YOUR WORTH

Karen Smith

"Sometimes our greatest act of bravery is simply saying *no more* to giving our value away to others."

Know Your Worth

Freedom, my heart whispered peacefully as I watched my boss from out of state unexpectedly stride through my office door that cold Friday morning in January. *No!* my stunned brain screamed. *You've got to be kidding me! After the nine years I've dedicated to this company?* My stomach felt like it dropped to my feet, and my breath caught tightly in my chest. I instantly knew what was about to transpire; it is simply the way letting you go is done when you work at the executive level in corporate America.

Our division was in the middle of a major restructuring, and I had been part of the strategic planning for pieces of the new business blueprint. I had already done the herculean work of physically closing one office and begun integrating two diverse and separate teams.

What had not been openly discussed was the way that the new structure would affect us as executive leaders. Although I had wondered in the back of my mind what might be coming, I reasoned there were more than enough teams and initiatives to lead and manage with the physical office moves, combining and blending teams, and leading change management efforts, all while still growing the business and the profits.

I had a very good personal track record and had been with the company for nine very productive years. I'd personally added over $1.4B (yep, billion) to the company's balance sheet and worked on projects all over the globe. I knew I delivered great value; it never even crossed my mind that I might not be included at the table going forward.

Despite my rapidly beating heart and knocking knees, I calmly welcomed my boss with a smile as I stood out by my team on the sales floor, conveying the attitude that I had been expecting him and all was well. He couldn't even meet my eyes as he asked if we could talk in my private office. I simply looked at him and said, "I'll get my things." He finally lifted his eyes to meet mine and then immediately looked away and walked toward my office. *He knew I knew.* Despite his outwardly calm body language, his energy clearly conveyed that he didn't want to be the one delivering the news.

I picked up my notebook, steadied my nerves with a few deep breaths, and walked purposefully toward my office. I breathed a prayer of "I trust you, Lord, whatever happens." My heart gently tugged with a second whisper of hope, *Freedom lies ahead!* An intuition flashed through my thoughts: *Will this be my launching point to finally leave corporate America to become an entrepreneur?*

My boss waited for me to be seated and, still not meeting my eyes, pulled out a folder and simply said in an impersonal monotone, "I'm here to tell you that your position has been eliminated." There it was . . . the knowledge and the glimmer of light on the horizon, but still, the awfulness of hearing the words spoken aloud and it actually happening. The energetic vibe I was receiving from him was out of character, like I had suddenly become a deadly poison and he had to get away as quickly as possible to avoid contamination. I had worked with him for many years and generally had a good and productive relationship with him.

He went through some details, which started setting off alarm bells in my head. After he finished, he looked up and said, "State law says we have to give you two months' notice because of your age." During his speech I said nothing, nor did I show any reaction. You simply couldn't show any weakness in executive positions, especially if you were a woman. I felt numb inside and completely invalidated. It felt like none of my hard work, leadership, sacrifices, and business growth had mattered to them. I could still hear him talking, but my mind was already moving into "solve" mode. It was surreal.

Deep in my heart I also sensed that it wouldn't matter if I had anything to say. They didn't want to hear me; they had never wanted to "hear" me. When I still didn't say anything or react, but continued to look steadily at him, he nervously blurted out, "Do you want to take the rest of the day off or go home now?" Why would he think I needed to go home? I wasn't about to break into a hysterical crying fit or explode in anger. The day's sales needed to be made and our customers taken care of. I was a high-performing executive leading a large net worth business unit who had worked in much harder circumstances than this! I heard myself say "No" even though my mind was already making a list of who I needed to call immediately and things I would need to do.

He offered me his hand and mumbled, "I'm sorry and I hope you understand."

My heart thought, *Why would I understand this? There is so much that is wrong on every level here.* I heard myself say, "Thank you and have a safe trip home." *Why am I still being so polite and kind after all they've done to me?* I determined in that very moment that I would maintain my integrity, character, and professionalism even if my company would not and did not.

He walked out my office door, quickly said goodbye to a couple of people as he tapped his watch and talked about catching a flight, and then walked out of our office. I could feel my team's eyes on my back as he left. That's right: he didn't even have the courage to stay and inform my team; he left that for me to do! *What a yellow-bellied coward*, I thought, disgusted. Little did I know it was a foreshadowing of things to come in the next few months.

I stayed in my office to catch my breath and calm my mind. Then "monkey brain" started kicking into high gear and dramatically overthinking.

How am I going to accomplish my goals or pay my bills? What will my family think? What should I do next? Should I walk out right now? For crying out loud, I've just built a brand-new house! How will I cover the mortgage? My faith whispered back, *Steady. God is always faithful, and He has a plan for you.*

The rest of the day and the weekend were a blur. My beloved twin sister and parents were wonderfully supportive, as was a CEO friend who responded to my texts with his own text back of "BEST.DAY.EVER" and "Fly baby Fly!" Their excitement around my newfound freedom solidified what my heart had continued to intuitively reinforce to me. The question became, would I *believe* my heart and trust God, no matter what happened?

LIONESS AWAKENING

The next few months became some of the toughest I had experienced in my working career. I never imagined that I would have to defend myself in the ways that I did. It sparked an awakening in me that I'm not sure could have come about in any other way.

The awakening began approximately a week after I received my termination notice. The call with Human Resources (HR) began awkwardly from a pretentious show of compassion. I knew the woman in HR and worked with her weekly; her behavior was uncalled for. Although normally quick in my thinking, I literally didn't even know what to say to her about the whole thing. Then one of my favorite scriptures, Joshua 1:9, filled my heart: "Have I not commanded you? Be strong and courageous. Do not be afraid; do not be discouraged, for the Lord your God will be with you wherever you go."

The HR professional started to go over the details of my severance package, and as I looked at the numbers, alarm bells went off in my head. My stomach dropped to my feet again. They were offering only one week of pay for each year I had worked for the company instead of the standard written policy of two weeks of pay per year of work. She kept babbling along, but my stunned brain and heart felt numb. My brain was screaming, *What is going on? Why are they offering me less than what the standard policy is?*

In that very moment, I had a lightning bolt of clarity and courage that became *the moment* that the lioness in me arose with a fierceness that almost scared me. These people were so morally bankrupt and devious that they were attempting to cheat me out of the standard offering from the company as a severance baseline! And, severances were often negotiated out to much more than the baseline! Mind you, I was a high-performing, respected employee with a solid reputation around the company. I had delivered massive value to the balance sheet, and I could articulate and prove that value.

Despite a rare anger rising into my throat, I was calm when I mentioned that the policy was two weeks of pay instead of one week. The woman from HR went dead silent and then gave a nervous, tittering giggle like a schoolgirl who had gotten caught. She hemmed and hawed for a few seconds and then said, "Oh, I think the policy was updated, but I'll double-check." I was irate. *How stupid or uninformed do they think I am?* I thought. *I look at those policies all the time! I would have been given an updated one if it had changed.* As an executive, you work closely with HR all the time as you manage your teams and business. A big change in policy would definitely have been given to us! As that thought scrolled through my mind, I had another awakening around how they perceived me. They thought that since I was generally nice, friendly, congenial, and adaptive that they could just steamroll me one more time.

In that very moment I decided that I would stand up for myself as I had never done before in my career. I no longer had anything to lose in the company. I would continue to be professional and maintain my integrity, but I would openly question everything, and I would not let them cheat me.

Sometimes our greatest act of bravery is simply saying *no more* to giving our value away to others. We must first recognize and cherish the fact that we have value simply because God chose to create us and has a plan for us. No person or career gives us our baseline value.

However, we live in a world that loves to tell us that our value comes from performing for love, career and financial success, building an influencer status, and other external factors such as a perfect body, relationships, our resume, and noticeable wealth.

In the week that followed my initial call with HR, they came back with an updated offer that included the correct severance amount. They offered no apology for what they had tried to do; they simply blamed a junior HR person for getting it wrong. If I had not stepped into my own bravery, I would have been intentionally cheated out of thousands of dollars. It was a major victory for my heart to know that my deep conviction had actually resulted in a tangible difference for my new future. It was incredibly empowering to finally stand up for myself! I was used to standing up for my team, our customers, and our business, but not for myself.

I had finally gotten some direction from my manager about who was taking over my team. Unfortunately, it still fell to me to tell my team what had happened. It was a stunningly egregious and unethical breach of leadership integrity. Normally, executives are walked out the door immediately after receiving their notice, and either HR or their manager stays and explains to the division what the next steps are and who the new leader is. In this situation, the cowardice of the HR and business leaders was nauseating and despicable. Why I did not stand up for myself and tell them that they needed to deliver the message themselves would be another growth lesson for me to integrate later. This felt like a deep low after the high of standing up for myself with the severance negotiation.

My team's reactions were understandably mixed; first they were puzzled, then they were shocked, and then they were questioning and fearing for their own positions. We had been verbally told that we were being blended with another team, but the actions we were seeing told a different story. I had no way of reassuring my team members about anything. To complicate matters, the person taking over for me seemed completely uninterested in getting to know the team or even engaging in the necessary work to take over. They refused to meet with me to go over the strategy, the budgets, and so on. My heart once again came to my rescue with wise counsel: *Be careful of the snake you cannot see.* Heeding that warning would stand me in good stead.

POWERFUL REALIZATIONS

The old me wanted to be extra helpful, to somehow prove that the business was making a mistake by letting me go. The new lioness realized that I was free to let go and watch the business continue where it would in the hands of the new leaders. I was no longer responsible for it — for what it created, what it delivered, or even whether it still existed in a month, in a year, or in ten years. Letting go of this weighty responsibility created a powerful shift in me. I realized that we don't actually leave a legacy in this type of work world. As you leave, the company will simply replace you with another person from the endless chain gang.

It was both a massive relief to let go and another lesson in courage that I needed to start embodying. I had spent my twenty-year career working extremely long hours, taking on difficult projects, moving all over the country away from my family, and, frankly, sacrificing myself and my dreams in the process. My work master had required everything I had; I complied because I often wasn't brave enough to see or stand up for my own worth and value. I had traded my time for money and was left with a short balance sheet. These realizations continued to feed that new lioness and strengthened me to say no to new opportunities that were offered in the company.

During all this time, I prayed about what to do next. I honestly didn't know what God had planned, but I knew He would eventually show me. I had made lists of possible options, but nothing really struck my heart. Logically I could easily get another corporate gig, but in my heart, I knew I couldn't do it again, especially after what I was going through. I wanted to be free, to create, to work with high-vibe people, and to share more of my giftings with the world. I also was tired.

This bravery resulted in a newfound self-assurance and courage that felt strong, peaceful, and solid, and even brought me some happiness despite an uncertain future.

Know Your Worth

I continued to go to work every day and behave in a professional manner and with a good attitude. However, I stopped performing for the business, chasing down the new leader, or responding to the demands of those still in power. The business was no longer mine to lead.

I noticed that the upper-level leaders saw this shift in me, and they began calling, digging for information about what my new path would be. One of our main competitors was two hours up the road, and I had worked for them before coming to my current company. I didn't realize how worried my current leaders were that I would go back to the competitor until they presented me with ridiculous demands in a non-disclosure agreement (NDA).

Normally NDAs are presented at the front of the severance package and basically are legally binding agreements preventing you from sharing any secret information from your current company with anyone else. They might also include a period of time that you can't work in your current industry.

Their NDA would have prevented me from working in my industry for *years*. I knew that no judge would enforce it, so I refused to sign it. When they tried to tie it as a condition of my severance package, I still refused to sign it. It was one more confirmation that this layoff was going to be a massive blessing in my life. If they thought I was so valuable to the competitor, why were they letting me go? I could energetically feel the power balance shifting slightly back to me. Bravery always has a higher vibration and result than fear or manipulation.

At home I continued to pray about which new direction God wanted me to go. I knew that my unspoken heart prayers for freedom were finally being answered. My soul knew I would not stay in corporate America; I had wanted to get out for a long time. The time for deliverance had come. New life awaited me. My courage would get another test as I sorted out what my heart wanted versus what other people and my logic advocated for.

NECESSARY ENDINGS

I knew that I was capable of being an entrepreneur, because I'd been dabbling in side businesses for years. I also came from a background of self-employed business owners and farmers, which gave me an awareness of what that life required. I was very aware that although someone might have business experience in corporate, being an entrepreneur is an entirely different reality that means wearing many hats, from CEO to janitor. I felt a multitude of emotions: excitement about new possibilities, self-doubt about starting all over again, apprehension around the unknown, and yet a deeply abiding peace from my faith in God.

As the last week of my corporate years came to a close, I received calls from other executives and those at the top of the house. One particular conversation offered me closure, perspective, and confirmation. The gentleman told me what he had observed in the previous couple of months. "You exhibited such a high level of integrity and professionalism; I was really impressed by that," he said. "I think we made a mistake in not keeping you, but we knew you'd be able to quickly adjust to a new opportunity better than other people we kept."

I was stunned as I listened to him; he clearly was not even listening to what he had just said! I was grateful he mirrored to me his perception that I had kept my integrity and character. I was even more grateful that I had trusted my intuition that this was no longer a good and honest place to work. What business will succeed if it prefers its lower-performing people over its best? It truly helped my brain come into final alignment with my heart energy. My life verse of scripture, Proverbs 3:5-6, flashed into my brain: "Trust in the Lord with all your heart and lean not on your own understanding; in all your ways submit to him, and he will make your paths straight." I had a blessed assurance that God's presence would always be with me as I journeyed on this new adventure.

As I hung up the phone, rather than be offended by his revealing words, my brave heart whispered back *Freedom*, so I walked out my office door and into that sweet freedom of new life adventure that awaited me.

A NEW LIFE

The following Sunday I was on a plane bound for Franklin, Tennessee, to be trained as a Dave Ramsey Master Financial Coach. In the last couple of weeks before I left corporate, I had finally decided, with the encouragement of others, to offer business and financial coaching and consulting.

I felt like this was a good way to link my current skills and future possibilities. I knew there was more to my future path, but I didn't know how to articulate it to people. It also gave me the freedom and flexibility with my time that I had longed for. I could work from anywhere I wanted to travel and with higher-consciousness clients.

I had followed Dave's money principles for years and had become debt-free except for my house. My dedication to completing this step in my financial life would be challenged over and over. As a single woman who was the sole breadwinner, I had to be willing to make sacrifices today in exchange for a more prosperous future. This freedom from debt became an integral centerpiece of my being able to leave corporate and embrace a new life as an entrepreneur.

I had been helping people and businesses with Dave's financial principles and the natural laws of money for a few years. I saw the transformative effect it had on people's lives and dreams. I especially noticed that employees who actively managed their personal money were much more likely to be good stewards at work with the company's balance sheet. They were more open to growth and change when the businesses demanded it. When people break the chains of the slavery of debt, they are empowered to chase their dreams, weather the storms of life, and, more importantly, be a genuine blessing to others.

I knew entrepreneurship would require a whole new me showing up every day. I needed to step into my brave to be free of my old baggage, the injustices, and unproductive beliefs. It was hard, messy, and exhausting at times.

One of the things we must be able to do as we change and grow is be brave enough to tell ourselves the truth. The freedom that comes from truth is incredibly powerful and life giving. To help a new garden flourish, you must remove the old, dead debris and prune back the unproductive that is blocking new growth.

I had worked with wise counselors and a dear mentor over the previous few years whose help was invaluable. My beloved mentor had opened new doors to me by teaching me about energy work and healing. I had been studying the energy of money and its influence on people's money stories for years. Intuitively I knew this was an idea that held deep promise for me.

I loved that she'd helped me energetically release old, trapped emotions, limiting beliefs, old stories, and mental and emotional blocks. I saw real change starting to blossom within myself. I had always had such a deep sense of unworthiness in my heart that despite my wonderful success, I often felt like I wouldn't be able to achieve my dreams or have the life I really wanted. This wise woman had spoken so much life into me and had even prophesied that someday I would be an energy healer. My heart was bursting with hope and joy upon hearing that. When your destiny is revealed, you will never be the same.

Of course, my monkey brain started chattering and telling me I couldn't do energy work. What would people think? How would the leaders and members of my church react? Little did I know that in just a few short years I would need every bit of courage I had and fully step into a full-time energy work practice that focused on serving businesses and individuals by pairing practical skills with energetic alignment for greater success in all areas.

Finding the courage to make changes and blossom into my own giftings caused me to learn how to embrace and enforce boundaries, to speak up for what I wanted as well as what I didn't want. I had to be brave enough to offer myself grace and love. I finally started telling people how I was really helping businesses and individuals transform by intuitively advising them on businesses, finances, and success through my energy modalities. Watching my amazing clients excel was so incredibly energizing and fulfilling that I woke up every morning excited to serve them.

Living from a place of courage also meant embracing a life that didn't look like a corporate executive's. It meant taking on the care of my eighty-five-year-old dad in my home after my mom passed away. It meant moving to a different state and working from home long before it was popular. Sometimes it has meant doing the farm chores before Zooming with the CEO of a business in another country. It meant developing multiple sources of income through three businesses so that I could build my life the way I wanted it to be. I became a director with a natural skin-care direct-sales company, had an Airbnb offering, taught classes on money consciousness and success principles, and sold products at my local farmers' markets.

I took courses and traveled to international seminars to learn from master teachers, including Bob Proctor. I continued to read voraciously, seek wise advisers and business partners, and try multitudes of ideas. Lastly, it meant finally being courageous enough to *commit* to a defined path, fully trusting being in alignment with God and His natural laws of success. Commitment has a powerful energy to it, and we must wisely engage in it in our relationships, our finances, and our businesses.

This journey of bravery also meant recovering from a lot of failure, roadblocks, financial gains and losses, global pandemics, constant change, and unexpected occurrences while my intuition continually reminded my heart to seek the Lord and freedom in every area.

Louisa May Alcott, a celebrated nineteenth-century novelist, perfectly expresses a major idea I was learning with this pithy yet poignant one-liner: "I am not afraid of storms, for I am learning to sail my ship."

Today, living courageously is a daily embrace of trusting God, allowing myself to fully receive and give, choosing what is right for my heart and in alignment with God, living out my callings, and showing others that they too can have this same freedom. What we often think might be the worst day of our life *can* turn out to be one of the best days of our new life.

Know Your Worth

ABOUT THE AUTHOR

KAREN SMITH

Karen grew up in the wild northern mountains of Colorado on a small rural farm. This started her life-long passion for all things agricultural and natural living. Today she continues to serve her beloved agrarian family as President of Colorado Cattlewomen, Inc. and helping her family on their ranch.

After university, Karen thrived as a corporate executive, but always felt the call to return to freedom of being an entrepreneur. She founded Pure Light Leadership where she specializes in the natural laws and energy of money, helping others create multiple sources of income, creating wealth and abundance mindsets and actions, and removing energetic blocks to success.

Karen is a Dave Ramsey Master Financial Coach and an energy healer as a Certified Emotion Code and Body Code Practitioner. She thoughtfully pairs the energetic with the practical to empower people to have freedom in all areas of their life. She is co-host of the Brilliant Horizons Leadership podcast which focuses on leadership, mindset, entrepreneurship, faith, energy and abundance.

You can find her inspiring others and creating a legacy of freedom at www.purelightabundance.com

Reach out and connect at:
linkedin.com/in/ksKarenSmith or kasmith1857@gmail.com

Chapter 8

RISE UP AND THRIVE

Dawn Loding

"We do not have to be a product of our upbringing."

Rise Up and Thrive

How did I get myself into this situation? I'm twenty-eight, divorced, and have two small boys. I am on my way to my second job, as a waitress, praying I make enough in tips to buy some groceries on the way home.

I just had a new table of twelve seated out on the patio. It's a beautiful Saturday afternoon, and the drinks will be plentiful for this crew, I am sure of it! I am grateful, because that means the tips will allow me to buy enough food for the whole week for the boys and me.

Struggle and living in survival mode have been common themes in my life. I am now fifty-three, but I only recognized this five years ago. Living in survival mode is a real thing. Our brains are wired at a very early age. I have heard it referred to as "a product of my raising." As a child and especially as a teen, all I wanted was to grow up and be able to create my own life. I knew I was a hard worker and that if I worked hard at something, it would pay off and I would find the path to a good life. Little did I know that that was *not* going to be as easy as I thought. But I knew it could be done! Right? And damn it, I was determined to do it. There had to be a better way to live than the one I knew, with its struggle, hardships, and lack. Lack of so much.

Looking back, I wondered how those people sitting at the patio table were able to afford all those drinks and all that food. They looked so happy, without a care in the world. I wanted to live like that. "Enough" was all I ever wanted, but until the past few years, it was as if someone had put all the "Good Life" instructions behind a brick wall, and every time I broke away some of it, another wall was behind it. Success was what I was striving for. I knew no one was going to do the work for me. I made the commitment to myself to figure it out on my own.

The struggle started very early for me. My parents were very young when they had me, and divorced before I was one. I was brought into my dad's larger family, where I was the first and only grandchild for about nine years. As I grew up, I became very close with my Papa and Nanny, my dad's parents. The bond I had with Papa was the most special one. He was my hero.

Life was definitely a lot harder back then, but the one thing I had with my grandparents was love. To this day, I love them very much and am extremely grateful for all they did to help raise me.

Even with all that love, I was moved around a lot. My parents did the best they could, but my dad ended up hitting the bottle, just trying to get through life. I spent my entire childhood and teen years pissed off at him. He embarrassed me time after time. I was so ashamed of him. I did not see him very often over the years, and when I did, I was not interested in anything he had to say. I was filled with so much anger. I wish I had let go of that anger before he passed so I could have gotten to know the person he was behind the drinking, but as a child, you just don't understand alcoholism. He passed away when I was nineteen and nine months pregnant with my first son.

My mom did the best she could as a young single mother in the seventies. She had several jobs, and we moved around a lot. We were really close, so when she hurt, I hurt. Sometimes it was as if we were growing up together. At one point, I counted the number of schools I had gone to before graduating high school and it was around fifteen. I went back to Papa and Nanny's quite often. I was always happy about that, but at the same time, I missed my mom unbelievably. I loved my mom, and when things were good, it was nice. It just didn't last for long.

My school days were pretty hard. I would often go to the nurse's office and complain of being sick, just so Papa would come and get me. I was bullied a lot, for whatever reason, and just wanted to be with my grandparents. I would give anything now to be in Papa's arms and hear him sing "You Are My Sunshine" one more time. He was the kind of man everyone wanted to be around. We used to say he had the gift of gab and that I got that gift from him, along with my love of animals. I have pet squirrels, and he had pet blue jays. Although they were wild animals, they trusted us completely and took nuts right from our hands. To this day, I believe it is a spiritual thing and a reminder that there is much more going on than what we know. I still have squirrels and often think of him as they take nuts from my hand.

My grandparents lived in a small two-bedroom house. I don't know how, but we were able to put thirty people in that house for holidays and sometimes sleep ten. They never had much money, but they had the basics — nice towels, bedding, and always something home-cooked sitting on the stove. Oh, and always a pitcher of sweet tea. I kept several of Nanny's pitchers when she passed away, and I keep fresh flowers in them on my table where I can see them and think of her. People were always welcome at their home, and they fed anyone who walked through the door.

I am very grateful for those memories. But when I was not with my grandparents, I had to go through some pretty rough stuff, which left me feeling abandoned and wondering what would be taken from me next. Those are issues that leave long-lasting emotional scars. The ones that show up in life on a regular basis. The ones I want to run and hide from.

When I was in sixth grade, my mom had to move to Wyoming to care for her sick mother. She took me with her. I was absolutely miserable. Shortly after the move, she let me go back to California and live with Papa and Nanny. That was great while it lasted. Two short years later, she showed up in California to get me. By then, I was in the eighth grade, and my mom had met a man who wanted us to be a family. I was torn. On one hand I thought, *Great, a real family, a mom and a dad, all living in the same house. A "normal" life.* On the other hand, I was doing well with Papa and Nanny and couldn't bear the thought of leaving my hometown and all of my family.

I went. I actually had no choice. I will never forget Papa and I both crying uncontrollably, on separate sides of the car window, as our car pulled away. It turned out to not be the dream family my mom and I thought it would be. Actually, that period of time left me with more scars than I could have imagined.

My family was always content with who they were and what they had. I was not. I wanted to *be* someone! I wanted every bit of good this life had to offer. My glass was always half full, even through the challenges. But as time went on, all I could find was the same thing I'd had growing up. In my twenties, my husband and I were doing the same thing I had been trying to get away from for so long: moving every year, changing jobs, fighting. It's not surprising that our marriage quickly ended in divorce. I was doing to my two boys exactly what my parents had done to me. It breaks my heart to even write about it, but it's true. I knew I had to find a way to stop the cycle my family had gone through for generations.

So there I was, a single mom, with two small sons and two jobs. This was my life. How was I ever going to make it better? How was I ever going to get ahead? I remember coming home one night from the restaurant and seeing an infomercial about becoming a real estate investor. I knew I could do that, if only I had the $199.99 they wanted for the program. I could barely make my car payment and pay the rent, so how could I do something like that? I had often thought that I would like to get my real estate license, but my grandmother always told me that was just a dream and what I needed was a real job, one with benefits and retirement. So I pushed the thought aside and stuck with what was "safe."

A short time later I met Kenny, now my husband of more than twenty years. We became friends, and my life started changing. After dating for three years, we married. That same year, Papa died. It was a year that changed my life in many different ways: so much good but also so much sadness. I was reminded that life is short and that things can change at the drop of a hat. All we can do is make it count.

Kenny had never been married and had no children. He took my two boys in like they were his own and loved them with all he had. They were only seven and nine at the time. He loved all three of us, and we became the family I had always dreamed of. We discussed having more children. It seems like that was all it took, because I was pregnant shortly after our wedding. I had some complications with my pregnancy and had to stop working, and was put on disability. I was told to take it easy and stay home. I am not a stay-at-home kind of person! I've been on the move since I was born; moving is pretty much in my blood. I thought, *What the heck am I going to do?*

Then I realized this was the perfect time to study and get my real estate license. Life is short, after all, and I really wanted this. Kenny knew I had always wanted to get my real estate license, and he believed in me and knew I could make it happen. He was my biggest fan. He really encouraged me, so we bought the books. Kenny was so supportive.

I studied and studied, and the baby got bigger and bigger. I was eight months along in my pregnancy and ready to take the real estate exam. I debated whether to take it before or after the baby was born. I was too impatient to wait, so I made the appointment. Kenny drove me the two hours to the city where the exams were administered. I remember it like it was last year. It was the middle of summer, in California, and the air-conditioning in the building where I was taking the exam had gone out. It was *hot*. I mean sweltering hot, and I was eight months pregnant! I could not concentrate. I thought for sure I had failed.

Unfortunately back then, they did not tell you the results after you took the test, so I had to go home and wait. Wait for a baby and wait for an answer to the fate of my future! Well, two weeks later, the mail came, and there it was: a letter with an answer inside. Was I going to be on the road to success or had I hit a dead end? My prayers were answered.

I *passed!* Full speed ahead! Now I just needed to have this baby and get to work.

When my baby boy was two weeks old, I headed to my job at a real estate office. *Oh my God, is this happening? Have I really done this? I felt so out of place.* My clothes were not fancy at all, and looking back, I'm sure I did not fit in. I had a two-week-old baby at home and was just a plain-Jane kind of girl, not some hot-shot real estate agent. But my thought was *Fake it till I make it.* I was determined. I knew I would never find the pot of gold at the end of the rainbow if I did not put myself out there in uncomfortable situations and do the work.

Well, it paid off! Jackpot! This was my gig! I had several contracts my first month. My first year was a hit. I remember going to an awards ceremony at a country club where I had once worked as a waitress, but this time I was a guest. I was dressed up and thought I was living the life I had always dreamed of.

Or was I?

Becoming a Realtor, in my mind, was my way of making sure I never had to struggle again. I was my own ticket to freedom: freedom from being at the mercy of others. I was in charge of my path. I was a survivor! I would never have to run again.

I thought all I had to do was make the money. I wasn't aware that no one had ever taught me how to manage it once I had it. Here again, "you are a product of your raising" showed up in my life. I didn't understand. I was making money, so why did I still not have enough?

Within that first year, we sold the moderate home we lived in and bought a big house in the country on two acres. By year three of our marriage, we had another baby, making our family complete with a total of four boys. We had managed to get by, pay the bills, but we were still living paycheck to paycheck. That is definitely a thing for real estate agents. Although the job brings some of the highest-paying commissions, many agents are poor money managers.

I started to notice who the responsible agents were — the few in the big offices who made it work. I asked myself, *What are they doing, and how do I do it?* I knew I needed to do it, but none of them would share what they were doing because of a real estate agent's most-feared word: *competition*. Don't give your secrets away, because if you do, they will take away your business. But then I asked myself, *Are they really making it work, or do they just make it look like they are?* We can only do so much business as an agent. There is only so much time in a day.

In 2006, my grandmother passed. It was time for us to get out of California and find a better life for our family. We decided to move to Texas. My husband had a great business opportunity, and I could get my license and do real estate there.

After doing a complete remodel and putting a lot of money into it, we sold our home in California. We were on our way and planning to close on the house in Texas within a few days. In the middle of our move to Texas, my phone rang one morning, bright and early. I thought, *This can't be good news.* It was the agent for the buyer of our home in California. The one we had just left. The one the buyers had put a $10,000 nonrefundable deposit on, saying yesterday we were good to go and would be closing the following day. Well, they canceled at the very last minute. What were we to do now?

I was in tears. My husband and I talked. Do we go back to California? Do we press on to Texas? It was a big decision to make, not only for our family but also for my in-laws, who were moving with us.

It was a big decision that was all about the money. What if we ran out of money? We were counting on the house closing and being able to use those funds to survive for a bit. We did have some savings, but not much, and we had no idea how many house payments we would have to cover until our house sold, in addition to paying for the house we were buying. I wasn't anywhere near getting my Texas real estate license. We were going to have to figure out how to make things work with just my husband's business opportunity and the small amount we had in savings.

We told ourselves that life is not about going backward, so we continued on to Texas. Looking back, I wonder if maybe we were supposed to stay in California. As it was, we had struggle after struggle in Texas for the next six years — we navigated the 2009 housing/market crash just after I got my Texas real estate license, we opened and failed miserably at a new business venture, and we finally sold our house in California but took a $250,000 loss.

In 2012, my husband and I had another one of those life-changing talks. We decided to start over, sell the house we could no longer afford, and stop operating a business that was running us into the ground. We decided we would rather downsize than continue to live the way we were. The challenge with our plan was that like many other people, we were upside down in our house: we owed more on the mortgage than the house was worth. After all we had endured, we were now going to have to sell through what's called a short sale and lose money on the house, too. The bank agreed to take what was offered, leaving us with zero profit. When I tell my real estate clients that I have been through it all and understand what they're going through, I truly mean it. We just knew we had to make the change, so we moved forward.

We found a great house to lease that sat on a hill with a view to die for. It was a beautiful area. Even though it was just a lease, we knew we could be happy there while we got back on our feet. We figured we could make it work for a couple of years. We loved that house. We thought that when the time was right, we would offer to purchase it. But that was not to be. After one year, the owner decided they wanted to move into it. We just couldn't seem to get ahead. We were displaced again.

We started to look for our forever home and eventually found our dream house — a small house in the country at the end of a cul-de-sac on two tree-filled acres. The only problem was that it wasn't for sale. It was all-original-1985-everything, but we really liked it and knew we could make it our own with some remodeling. The house was in the neighborhood next to the one we were leasing in. I had gone out walking every day and dreamed of owning one of the homes in the area. The birds and deer were plentiful, and the squirrels ran about.

One day, when I was out for my daily walk, I left a note on the door: "We're interested in buying this home." I knew it was vacant, since a friend in the neighborhood had told me the owner had just passed away. We finally connected with the owner's son, and Kenny and I were able to make an offer that was accepted. Wow, this was it! We had finally made it!

But wait a minute: how successful was I, really? I was working nonstop, every weekday and almost every weekend. I rarely had a day off. When you have five to ten contracts at a time, the phone never stops ringing. That's a sign of success, right? By this time, I was in my late forties, watching my life fly by. My children were growing up fast. The struggles were still coming. If I wasn't handling real estate deals, I was consumed with the bills to pay; if not with the bills, I needed

Rise Up and Thrive

to spend time with the kids. It's a wonder Kenny and I have made it through this life.

One day I asked myself, *Where am I and what am I doing?* I had no retirement; by now, my husband had a small one, but I had little to nothing to show for all my hard work. I was still working paycheck to paycheck. Yes, the checks were for higher amounts, and there were more of them, but as your real estate business grows, so do the expenses. You need a larger office to fit more people, and you pay for more leads for your team. And the most important part is the coaching you pay for as a high-producing agent.

The expenses continued to grow. I kept working harder, but I wasn't working smarter! I was not where I wanted to be. Something was missing, but I had no idea what it was. I was not getting any younger, and I was still not living the good life I used to dream of. I had read many books on how to get to the top of the ladder and be successful. So why couldn't I feel like a success?

Honestly, all I felt was fear. My biggest fear was that I would lose all this success. Did I have it or not? My childhood kept creeping up on me. Who would come to take this away?

Was it my business? Was it me? What was I doing wrong or not doing? I was not happy, but I was successful. I knew there was more. I had to figure this out. I always found myself asking, *What is missing? Why can't I find some peace?* I would wake up in the morning, and the first feeling I had was fear. I felt as though I was going to lose something, like someone would take it from me. I was living with anxiety, worry, doubt, and fear on a daily basis.

I had spent my life chasing something. Success. Happiness. Love. Something I felt everyone but me had. But here's the thing: I did have it.

- I had passed the real estate exam for two different states, California and Texas.
- I was a successful real estate agent.
- I got to move to Texas.
- I had a wonderful family.
- I had lived in beautiful homes my entire adult life.
- I had an amazing group of friends.
- I had a husband who loved me, and four amazing sons, two beautiful daughters-in-law, and seven grandsons . . . so far.

My life was a fairy tale to some people. At times I felt really bad for complaining or thinking there should be more to life. But I just could not shake the feeling of wanting more. I felt like a dog chasing his tail.

One day I was talking to a good friend of mine, Sheila, who told me about a new national virtual real estate company with which she had become involved. I saw her on social media talking about how her life was changing and how she was experiencing so many great things. My first thought was *It's a real estate company. How can it change your life?* She sent me a video and told me to watch it. Not wanting to go through the trouble of making a move, I continued to watch her from afar. I was actually getting a little jealous of all her stories of success and doubting it was all true. However, I knew her, and I knew she was a very responsible and experienced agent.

I asked her what was so different about her work life now. She said, "I just can't explain it, but I feel like I am part of something bigger. This is the first virtual, all-online real estate company, and not only that, but they also offer multiple streams of income within the company for the agents." She said she felt like she was helping to build something for the future. The way the company is built is for the success of the real estate agent! Not just the broker. Agents actually have a chance to build wealth with the systems the company has in place.

I remember the day I finally watched the video. It took me six months to get around to doing it. But I woke up one Saturday morning and walked outside and sensed something. I'm not really sure what it was, but I suddenly thought, *What if I have worked my whole life for a moment, and I missed the moment?* Was I being invited to be part of something that I was going to pass up? There was some kind of urge to go watch that video. So that is exactly what I did. I could not believe what I was learning about this company. It sounded too good to be true. Multiple streams of income! I had read about that in books, but I was not sure what it looked like, much less how I could ever achieve it. How can anyone have time to do anything but sell real estate when it takes up all of your time?

My husband is the opposite of me. If I am on a fence about to jump, he's the one to help me off the fence and back to reality. He is much more of a realist than I am. Some would say I am a dreamer. I would say I make my dreams come true. So, I took my laptop to him and said, "Can you please watch this video about a new real estate company I am considering?"

He watched it, closed the laptop and said, "You need to go there ASAP." What?? I thought he would talk me out of it. I got so excited — a feeling I had not had in a while! I was taking a leap. A leap of faith. And it was exhilarating! I had no idea what was about to happen in my life. And my friend Sheila was right: it was something I could not explain.

I was at my new company within weeks.

The company had fewer than three thousand agents when I signed up, and I don't think a single one of them was in my town. I was like a pioneer, and I loved it. I was planning and working and figuring out all this new technology. It was fun and a bit scary at the same time. In February, the company was holding a national event in San Diego, California, just hours from where my family lived, including my two oldest sons. I thought I would fly out there, go to the event, and then take the train to my hometown to spend a few days with family — a celebration of my new venture.

So off I went to San Diego. I had never flown anywhere to go to a national event for any of the companies I had been with, so this was new. But Sheila had told me how important it was to go to these events. And from this point forward, I was doing whatever she suggested. I was a combination of nerves and excitement on the plane. Then, I had to figure out the Uber app to get to the hotel on Coronado Island. So many new things, but I was up for the challenge.

I arrived at the hotel, got settled in my room, and looked out the window and thought, *Oh my God, what have I done?* I felt like I was out of my league. I cried. I started to get fearful and doubt myself. It was so scary. *I don't belong here* was all I could think.

Then I decided to touch up my makeup, go check out the hotel, and put my big-girl panties on! So I did. Still feeling like a fish out of water, I walked down to the area that went out to a pool. I saw a group of about twenty women with eXp lanyards around their necks, and a sign that said "eXp Power Girls." I stood about thirty feet away and just watched in awe. These women had their act together. They were all happy and laughing and seemed to be living the good life. Then one of them walked over to me. "Are you in the Power Girls group?" she asked.

"No," I said. "What are the Power Girls?"

"We're a group of women at eXp who are all about empowering, uplifting, and welcoming other women to eXp."

I said it sounded amazing and then asked, "How do I get in?"

"You're in!" she said. "Come on!" She pulled me over to the larger group and introduced me to a couple of the women. They were all so adorable and so welcoming! I am still friends with these women to this day. I knew I was in the right place. This was just the beginning of many changes. I now knew what Sheila meant by "it's hard to explain."

So many things in my life started to change. It was as if my whole world was opening up. Instead of living my life in my small city, I was being exposed to the entire country. I was having weekly meetings with women from all over the country — not just real estate agents but entrepreneurs. I would spend my time not only working on my real estate business, but also building much more, as a business owner. Building my team. Building wealth. Building the Power Girls group. I have learned so much! In fact, I am now the national education director for the Power Girls group, and I have found my place helping other women feel welcome.

I was stepping into my vision, and through that I was able to attract the people meant to be in my path. I just needed to show up. I'm now on a playing field where people who have gone before me are willing to share all of their accomplishments with me. I found a productivity coach who helped me work through many of the issues I had from my childhood trauma. I was not aware of how it can affect our day-to-day work. She gave me the right tools to use and helped me understand healing. I started to feel whole.

I now have six streams of income, savings, and investments. I know how to roll with the punches the real estate industry throws at us. I have learned how to play a bigger game! I was able to expand my way of thinking by expanding my circle. And wow, how my circle has grown over the past several years! I know how common it is, as a woman, to find myself in a pit of doubt and fear, to be sad and scared. But the difference is that I now know how to pull myself out of it — immediately.

I have spent my life chasing money. But I finally shifted from focusing on how little money I had to realizing I could simply focus on what makes me happy. There will always be bills. I can learn how to manage money better, but I am no longer chasing it.

Much of my story is about shifting my mindset. Our minds are very intricate things. You can change the way you think, but it is something no one else can do for you, and it is a process — one worth every bit of the work it takes.

We do not have to be a product of our raising. I know there is much more to life than chasing the dream. There is living the dream. And I am finally able to do it. I am so grateful I never stopped searching for more. I am so grateful for my perseverance. I am so grateful for all the lessons life handed me. My hope for you is that if you feel like you don't belong, you'll just show up anyway.

Maybe it is where you were meant to be all along.

ABOUT THE AUTHOR

DAWN LODING

From an early age, Dawn knew she wanted to do something special in life, however the cards were stacked against her.

Finally, at the age of 32, she was able to get her Real Estate license and start living the way she had always dreamed of— or so she thought. She was on the right path, but carried a predesigned set of beliefs from her childhood.

Today, after 20 years of coaching, training and reading she has unlocked those beliefs and implemented a new mindset. Dawn believes this is an ongoing way of life if you want change. We must find a place of flow and engage with our best selves every day. Only then can we put ourselves out there for the world to meet.

Having broken that cycle and now living a life of freedom, she has made it her life's mission to help others with her signature training course, Freedom to Flourish in Real Estate. Learn more at www.dawnloding.com

Chapter 9

CLAIM YOUR DREAMS

Odeta Pine

"Anything worthwhile takes solid focus, energy, dedication, and sacrifice."

The view of the mountaintop from that tiny rectangle-shaped balcony window of our tiny apartment was always breathtaking. It was the way the sun always hit the slopes and the mesmerizing shade patterns it created as the day went by. My favorite part of the day was when the sun lit the mountain on fire, and all I could think about was how it would feel to be a bird flying over the mountaintop, slowly making my way down the mountain as the sun made its way down to the west. Often I would share that moment with my mom, who sat at her own tiny window next to mine. We would sit there for hours in silence, admiring the view. I would wonder what she was thinking, and I knew that as it got a bit darker, she would say, "Time to go — shut the window."

That window was my home for a long time during and after the 1997 civil war — the war that locked us in and dictated we stay inside. If we went somewhere, we were always supervised by our mom or dad, or both. We were told to trust no one but our parents. That small window was the only opportunity to look at the view, to dream about "another life" far away from the reality.

It was a Thursday night in January 1997, and my parents and I were walking back from visiting one of our family friends. I remember holding my dad's hand, looking up into the sky and seeing faraway sparkles and loud sounds, almost like a broken airplane was flying close above us. We didn't know what it was then, but we found out the next day.

It was the beginning of Albania's 1997 civil war — a time of chaos, uncertainty, prostitution, kidnapping, corruption, and killings. The war was sparked by the dramatic rise and collapse of several pyramid schemes. At the peak of these schemes, the nominal value of their liability was almost half of the country's GDP, and almost two-thirds of Albanians invested in them, having just gotten out of a long dictatorship. The schemes collapsed, uncontained rioting hit, the government fell, criminal gangs took over, and the country descended into anarchy.

That was the beginning of our family being pulled apart — a long time of hard sacrifices made. No one was safe going anywhere, and people were shot left and right on the streets. I remember we had to be home by five, six at the latest — right before it was dark — and I felt trapped and hated life. As a kid I couldn't play outside and see my friends even though that's what a ten- year-old wants to do most. This was what life looked like from those tiny balcony windows my mom and I often stared out of. We would get lost for hours looking at that mountain view — the only view we could enjoy — and wonder about another life out there.

I don't know how my parents felt, but I do remember they decided to get my sister out of Albania, and they did. She came to the United States in 1999 via a high school exchange program and stayed and finished college. We talked only over the phone. We always talked about being together as a family one day, and looked forward to it.

The war was over, but the situation was not good. I had no future in Albania, and my parents had a plan to get me out as well. I remember them talking a lot about going to the United States one day and the American Dream. I felt I had no say in my future. I wanted the American Dream, but I wasn't really the one choosing it for me. It was what they had done for my sister, and it was what felt safe and like the best thing they could do for us as parents. They didn't know better — they just knew I would have no future in Albania.

In 2002, I got accepted to one of the most prestigious English-speaking high schools in Korçë, Albania — Kolegji Preka. I had the best scores on the math and English tests. I was good in math and physics, and of course I knew English, because that was the way out of Albania. My high school years were the best when I was in school, but when I wasn't there, I still couldn't go anywhere by myself. I had to be home by a certain time, and my parents accompanied me everywhere. I mean, a teenager going with her parents everywhere . . . I always felt trapped and had to do what everyone else told me to do.

I graduated from high school with all As, and the time to apply for college came. I wasn't asked where I wanted to go, what I wanted to do, or which college I wanted to attend. I clearly remember the phone call from my sister saying she had applied to all these colleges in Boston, Massachusetts, and that I had to submit all this paperwork, and essays and achievements. So, I did. I did it not because it was what I wanted but because it was the way out toward the American Dream and our family reunion after all those years apart.

I remember saying in my head, *Why would I get a visa?!* Everyone would talk about how hard it was to get a visa and about the scary high wall surrounding the U.S. embassy in Tirana.

Albanians were denied the right to visit the United States, and we weren't to even think about going to college there. We were denied that opportunity because we were a corrupt and poor country, and the thinking was that if we went and visited, we would stay. A lot of Albanians did stay, not because they wanted to be in the United States illegally, but because they had escaped a horrible, trapped, poor life. They were looking for a better opportunity and, most importantly, freedom. We were all constantly chasing freedom in every sense of the word. My view of the mountain from that tiny balcony window was one of the million views that pushed and kept millions of Albanians going and chasing their freedom and that life far away from reality.

I got accepted to all the colleges I applied to and got scholarships to all of them, but my parents and my sister picked Simmons College because it was a very prestigious women's school (no men as a distraction) and offered the highest scholarship, which meant my parents didn't have to pay much. My parents had no financial freedom, and the saddest part was that they were both doctors and the most honest and hardworking people I had ever met.

I finally had an interview scheduled at the U.S. embassy in Tirana to get a visa, and went there in June 2006. I saw the high concrete walls surrounding the building — the scary but also dreamy walls Albanians would talk about all the time. As I walked in and sat down, I kept telling myself, *This is a waste of my time. I have a final tomorrow. I have to drive four hours back home and need to prepare for my college entrance exam in Tirana. What am I doing here? I won't get a visa.* I was anxious but also curious to know what would happen. I was taking time away from my exam preparation and felt I was doing it to make my parents and my sister happy. I did believe in a faraway, remote-from-reality American Dream — but really what I'd dreamed about while staring out the balcony window at the beautiful mountain and the bird flying over was freedom.

So, there I was, two questions into the interview when I was told, "Welcome to the United States of America!" I looked down, and then I looked up to the woman with the biggest smile and shiny eyes. I just stared at her for a bit and said, "Thank you." The sweet, nice woman — was she fake? She couldn't be American! I mean, she was the nicest and most smiley person I have ever met in my life! She lit up the room so that even the room wasn't as scary and dark as people had made it sound. She was American and different in the greatest way possible. My jaw dropped in disbelief, and my heart raced. I clearly remember telling myself, *This wasn't as bad as every Albanian said it was going to be. I got a visa, and I am going to live the American Dream, make it happen, be with my sister, and, most importantly, decide from now on what I will do with my life.*

It felt so *good* feeling that way. It was a moment of ecstasy, and I felt *free* just thinking about being in the United States. I celebrated my nineteenth birthday in July, and my parents got me a one-way ticket to Boston and prepared to send me off with a suitcase and some money that next month.

It was a long, silent, five-hour drive from Korçë, my hometown, to Tirana International Airport Nënë in August 2006. There was nothing nice about the drive, although the scenery — mountains, lakes, hills, valleys, and rivers — was beautiful. What made it so bad? It was the dark, not-wanting-to-say-goodbye feelings inside. I was sad to leave my parents — I mean, they wouldn't have any children left at home anymore. I knew my mom wouldn't have anyone with whom to look out the tiny balcony window or watch TV, or to help her with chores. It would be so lonely for her, and my heart was just breaking and breaking the more I thought about it. They had two girls they loved so much, and they had chosen to send them away.

When it was time to say goodbye, we hugged, and I remember fighting hard not to cry. I can still see my mom holding it together, both of us probably thinking, *I can't make her cry. I don't want her to feel bad and feel like she is giving me the last hug and goodbye* because we really didn't know what the future held, we didn't know when we would all be together again. I kept thinking, *There is no way back to that window anymore. I must climb up the mountain and onto this airplane and do my best to come back to hug my parents again sooner rather than later and just be with them and enjoy a free, relaxing time without running away or being locked down.*

My American Dream began the moment I stepped onto that plane. I had never been on a plane before — this was my first time. I was so excited but also so nervous. I was so scared but so happy. I was trying something new, and it felt awesome, and for the first time in my life I was doing something alone — my parents were not beside me as they always had been through the years. It took me a long time to get used to not having my parents next to me all the time — it was by far the biggest adjustment I had to make. I was finally leaving behind my war-torn country and, most importantly, that tiny balcony window.

I started school in September at Simmons College, and oh boy — where do I begin. The first day was a total mess. I felt lost and alone. I cried in the bathroom during breaks between classes. I knew English, but the British version, not the American one. It was hard to understand the professors, let alone get up and introduce myself with my thick Albanian-British accent. I went to the cafeteria but had no idea what to do. The place was huge. I didn't know how to pay for the food, and mind you, I had no cash that day. I got so overwhelmed that I literally ran out and starved myself until I got home at my sister's.

The food was a very big change for me, and I gained almost forty pounds my first month in shock. I had never had fast food, Chinese food, or Indian food. I had no concept of "snacking" and had never seen such big meal portions in my life! I was wowed that I was trying all these different kinds of foods and, more importantly, wowed by the diverse people in my classes. I had come from a war-torn place, isolated from the rest of the world, and here I was, trying the most amazing food and meeting the most diverse and cool people I had ever seen. It was like daydreaming but real, if that makes sense.

Life was good, but I was lonely. I struggled making friends at school that first year, and I remember calling my parents every day, crying that I wanted to go back and that I hated it here. Why did I stay? Well, because I didn't want to go back to the tiny balcony window and having my parents take me everywhere. I was an adult and strong and vowed that I

Claim Your Dreams

would never allow myself to go back to what I had been sent away from. It seemed like everyone was running all day long to get somewhere — they were always in a rush. This was the fast-paced American lifestyle all Albanian immigrants talked about. It wasn't my hometown where I knew everyone and talked to everyone. This was a good thing, because I couldn't stand everyone being up in my business back home. I felt free of that in a way, and I liked it, but it took me some time to adjust.

Somehow, despite all the challenges, I kept focused, and it was that window and the mountain view that kept me going. It was also my parents, who kept me pushing to hang in there. I did, and I made it out successfully. I graduated from Simmons College and got my first job at a software tech start-up out of Waltham, Massachusetts. That was a first dream job that led me to many other opportunities down the road.

I remember the day I got my first bi-weekly paycheck thinking, *I'm richer than my parents, I am financially free, and I will not ever be like them financially*! I kissed that paycheck and promised myself I would keep making it bigger and bigger over the years until I had my own business and could give that feeling to others who didn't have it. I wasn't going back at that point. I was pushing forward harder, stronger, and happier than ever.

I moved to Austin, Texas, in 2013 to help with the new office setup for the start-up I worked for — the same one where

I had my first job. I grew within the company, and so did the money and the opportunities. Moving to Austin was the best decision I made, because it was home, yet not the tiny balcony window. It was the place where I felt at home because people were so nice and helpful. They took the time to relax and get to know me and have a quick coffee or beer. It was the place where the American Dream came true in all aspects, and I started enjoying that mountain view I had daydreamed about from that balcony window for so long.

I got my citizenship in San Antonio, Texas. The process was long and expensive but so rewarding at the end. It was sad in a way, too, because I had to give up my Albanian citizenship, and I loved my country so much. I was in love with Albania, its people, and its beautiful mountains, lakes, waterfalls, and rivers, plus my parents were there. I was completely transitioning, going from a war-torn society to a freedom-based America. It was hard — I felt I was betraying my country and my roots — but then I kept thinking that the United States had given me more than my country ever had. This country gave me freedom — the freedom to walk by myself at any time of the day, freedom of speech, financial freedom, and opportunities — something people should have by birth in their own country and not have taken away. This was the country I wanted to be a citizen of and a proud one in every way.

After a long interview process, the moment I had so longed for was here — taking the Oath of Allegiance. I will never forget the goose bumps, followed by the tears and the pride I felt as I kept saying the oath out loud:

"I hereby declare, on oath, that I absolutely and entirely renounce and abjure all allegiance and fidelity to any foreign prince, potentate, state, or sovereignty, of whom or which I have heretofore been a subject or citizen; that I will support and defend the Constitution and laws of the United States of America against all enemies, foreign and domestic; that I will bear true faith and allegiance to the same; that I will bear arms on behalf of the United States when required by the law; that I will perform noncombatant service in the Armed Forces of the United States when required by the law; that I will perform work of national importance under civilian direction when required by the law; and that I take this obligation freely, without any mental reservation or purpose of evasion; so help me God."

I had never felt like or even thought about fighting for my own country, but I did for the United States of America that day. I am a proud Albanian and love my country and my culture, and I will never forget where I come from. But more importantly, I am a proud American as well. I truly felt and meant all of the oath — I truly would give it all for this country, because it has given me everything that I never had and that my country never gave me: freedom. After taking the oath and feeling so much pride, I kept thinking about how lucky Americans are to be free by birth, to be well protected and given so much freedom and so many opportunities to reach up high, wherever their dreams and wishes take them.

They can make dreams come true in a much easier and less sacrificial way because they were born here and given the best chance in life by birth!

The journey kept going and the American Dream kept happening. The American Dream meant freedom for me, but I learned that it was even more than that. As time passed, I grew as a person, and I learned a lot of hard lessons in both my business life and personally.

Growing up in Albania it was shameful to like a boy in high school or even college, and if you dated him, you were stuck with him. You would marry him even if it wasn't a good match, and you would make it work and stick it out no matter what. It was the "rule," which is crazy when you think about it. Not a lot of Americans understand this. When I got to the States, I knew nothing about relationships and therefore made the biggest mistake in my life: I married someone who didn't deserve me. He wouldn't let me grow professionally or personally, and it was awful. I got out of it after eight long years and met the man of my dreams in Austin — Dan. Dan was kind, sweet, and a true gentleman. Most importantly, Dan was a dreamer, and he was an American.

We started dating, and as we got to know each other better, I realized that although he represented the American Dream, I couldn't figure out in what way. I was unsure and anxious, with my walls up and trust issues. But I let go of my high-up walls and started to give him glimpses of my true self. Because I had failed once at a marriage, it was very challenging for me to let go and truly be myself with Dan. I didn't want to disappoint my parents again, especially my dad, but as time passed, we became closer and closer. I started loving him, and he stuck by me the whole time because he knew I was special. He didn't have to tell me about it; he showed me — he stayed.

We had five dogs, and each one of them with their unique bark, character, cuddle, and tail wiggling was special and brought us even closer. Albanians don't have dogs as pets, let alone five of them in an apartment. There were seven of us total! I still remember the night we were hanging out in our tiny little apartment with the five dogs cuddling on top of us when Dan opened his laptop. He filed the LLC paperwork for G7 Tech, my start-up, for me and said loudly, "You are meant to do this, and I know you can do it. I will support you until it is doing great, and will be here every step of the way."

We built a house together and weren't even married — something my culture wouldn't allow. Was I crazy? What was wrong with me? I constantly doubted myself and felt confused, but somehow, I also felt happy and at peace. When we bought our second house together, we still weren't married — we were happy, and that was all that mattered.

G7 Tech is growing in an amazing way every single day. I've done it with the best man by my side and full belief in myself. I stepped into my brave, and no one could stop me. I now have my citizenship, my business, my dream man, my dogs, our two huge, fun cars, and, most importantly, my beautiful baby boy, Odin, born in 2021. I have it all — the American Dream.

This was my quest for freedom. Life is a demanding journey. I might have not known the way my journey was going to unfold, but that mountain view and the tiny balcony window kept me focused. I became the bold eagle flying over the mountaintop. I enjoy the beautiful view as the sun sets every single day, and it doesn't stop there. I have plans, and I have other, higher mountains to fly over. It doesn't matter how high they might get; the mountain view and the tiny balcony window will still keep me going.

Life rewards those who are truly willing to keep pushing themselves no matter what limits, obstacles, challenges, and insecure feelings are presented to them. Always remember what got you to take the journey you decided to take and that anything worthwhile takes solid focus, energy, dedication, and sacrifice. Be proud to be an American and share that pride and love for America, because it is the land of freedom and opportunities and so awesome to be given that by birth.

ABOUT THE AUTHOR

ODETA PINE

Odeta Pine is a rare woman founder in the tech world. She brings a talent and passion for making technology more human to empower innovation in the companies she works with.

Part of a close-knit family, Odeta grew up in Korçë Albania, a small town rich in people and culture. Despite the chaos and poverty of growing up in the midst of a brutal civil war, Odeta's family actively worked to support her love of mathematics which sprouted into numerous awards and recognition in national mathematics & physics competitions.

In 2006, Odeta followed her sister to the United States with a suitcase and a goal to build her own business and live the American Dream. In 2015, after six years in a variety of positions and roles in the technology world, she recognized that dream as she launched her business, G7 Tech Services, "to provide tailored technology solutions across the Americas!"

Learn more at: www.theodetapine.com

ELEVATE YOUR VOICE

Elevate Your Voice is book one of the LIGHTbeamers Book Series.

In addition to April Adams Pertuis it features the 'voices' of these empowering women: Julia Barton, Becky Burroughs, Kristy Castilleja, Dr. Brittany Clayborne, Tessa Kidd, Marie Masse, Pamela Meadows, Sheryl Morley, Penny Pereboom, Leanne Smith, Deb Cummins Stellato, Stephanie Talia, and Kofi Williams.

Meet 14 women who faced challenges —from heart failure at 29 to the end of a 40-year marriage—and not only lived to tell about them but found their voices and used them to shape a new sense of purpose. One lost both parents within a year. One suffered from devastating postpartum depression. One struggled all her life to fit in and felt like she hadn't succeeded at anything—ever. Others questioned their faith, drove themselves to exhaustion in their quest to prove their worth, or realized that in spite of "having it all," they still felt an aching emptiness. Yet each of these women discovered she had something to say and created a richer, more meaningful life for herself. And each learned about the healing power of sharing her journey with other women. In telling their stories, they offer hope to every woman searching for change and longing to set her own voice free.

Read the first chapter on the pages that follow then purchase your copy on Amazon.

Chapter 1

STAND UP FOR YOURSELF

April Adams Pertuis

"It was about discovering my true value, and in finding that, I found my voice."

There have been a whole bunch of Sams in my career. I call them Sams, named after the original Sam who entered my life while I was making my way through journalism school. Sam was a student in the broadcasting program where I was enrolled. I'm not even sure how we first became friends. I just remember him being a likable guy. He was outgoing and good-looking, and others seemed to like him as well.

Sam befriended me. We were both go-getters and eager to perform at the top of our class. He complimented me and encouraged me as we dove deep into broadcasting projects like news gathering, video production, and editing. But as time went on, Sam's dark side showed up. If I was chosen to direct the team or to take the spotlight, Sam's claws came out. He'd try to undermine my decisions in an attempt to make me question my ideas. Or he'd give (un)constructive criticism in the guise of trying to help me be better.

After a few months of this, I grew tired of Sam. He frustrated me. I struggled to find ways to respond to his remarks without fueling his fire. He had a smooth way of turning the tables on me and making me feel small and helpless. I felt impeded. Silenced. Voiceless. When I looked at him, all I could see was an insurmountable roadblock in my way. No matter which direction I chose, he'd show up, and I'd have to figure out how to navigate around him. He became an omnipresent figure in my day. I dreaded walking into the journalism department (a place I had once loved) because I knew he'd be there. The worst was when we were alone, working extra hours on a project; his aggression was always on display when others weren't around to witness it.

I had never met a guy like Sam before. He was manipulative, undermining, and smooth. He threw me off my game, leaving me feeling incapable in many ways. Some days, I'd end up utterly despondent and broken, curled up in tears in my dorm room after class.

Finally, I'd had enough. I realized it was either Sam or my career . . . and no way in hell was I choosing Sam. I had a really great relationship with the two department heads—two men I greatly respected and admired. Nervously, I went to them and asked for help. I explained how Sam was causing me stress with his bullying tactics and aggression. I felt disempowered when he was around. I needed someone to intervene. I hadn't learned how to deal with a narcissist in my life yet. I was twenty-three. Sam was my training ground.

Things turned ugly.

Sam was approached about my complaints, and boy oh boy, did he want to make me pay.

It all came to a head one day when a bunch of students, including Sam and me, were sitting outside the studio after class. Our professors were handing out assignments, delegating roles in the next newscast we were to produce for the school. I was assigned a leading role, and Sam was assigned to a supporting role on my team. Almost simultaneously, we both protested. Sam couldn't stand the thought of me leading him, and I couldn't bear another minute of his vitriol as my teammate.

An argument between the two of us erupted in front of our classmates and our professors. Sam took every complaint of mine and twisted and turned it around like a pretzel and pointed all blame back on me.

Basically, it was all my fault he was an asshole.

One of the department heads stepped in. He pointed at Sam and told him he was out of line. He could either accept the role and work with me in compliance or remove himself from the show altogether. Sam chose the latter.

By now, I was sick to my stomach. I knew he wasn't going away that easily.

After we'd been dismissed, I left the building. Sam followed me. From behind, I could hear him calling out my name. "April, stop! Come back here. I want to talk to you!"

I ignored him and kept walking to my car.

His commands got louder and more demanding: "Stop right now. Listen to me!"

No I won't, Sam. I'm done with you! I thought, and I kept walking until I got to my car.

Sam was fast. Before I could open my door all the way, he was there slamming it shut, pinning me between him and the car.

In my face, he yelled at me. *"I said I want to talk to you!"*

"I don't want to talk to you, Sam. I said what I had to say back there in the studio. I'm done."

I tried to remain calm, but I could feel myself slipping. My neck was turning red, and I could feel my throat closing up. The burning feeling of tears hinted on the backside of my eyes.

I wanted to shove him out of my way, but Sam towered over me. He was not a small man. He was burly, strong, and physical. His face was red with anger.

At that moment, I was *done* giving all my power away to him. I'd spent months in utter anguish over his tirades, snide remarks, and criticism that came in the guise of trying to make me a better journalist. Time and time again, I'd go home at the end of class feeling defeated and voiceless. Sam's remarks would sting, and they made me question my ability to direct and lead a team. If I couldn't manage Sam, how was I going to lead production teams in the future? I had lost sleep, my appetite, and many tears over his presence in my life.

I had no more energy for him.

Standing in the parking lot, with Sam's hand on my door preventing me from leaving, I looked him directly in the eyes and said, "Sam, get your hand off my door. You either get away from me right now, or I'm going back into the studio to report you. This ends today. I am not your friend. We are done here."

Despite my best attempt to stay calm and exude confidence in that moment, I was shaking.

I wanted to throw up.

This man literally made me sick to my stomach.

I couldn't believe I was under this much stress over a guy with whom I had absolutely no connection other than the fact that we both happened to be at the same school, taking the same classes, trying to get a degree in the same field. We both wanted to be journalists.

For some reason, I was a threat to him. It was like there was only ever going to be *one job* available for both of us, and he was putting us through some sort of a Darwinian fight to see who was going to come out on top.

He exerted his power over me to make himself feel better. And he probably succeeded, because I know for sure I always felt worse after being around him.

Sam stared at me. I stared back at him, refusing to look away. I could feel myself slipping; I was forcing back tears while silently willing him away with every ounce of energy in my body.

He removed his hand from my door, and I got in my car and drove away. I never spoke to him again.

It's been over twenty-five years, and I've never forgotten him.

Unfortunately, there were many more Sams to come in my career.

That was just a warm-up.

At my last job in broadcasting, I worked as a weekday news reporter and weekend anchor at a CBS affiliate in Arkansas. I was up for a promotion to a full-time weekday anchor position. After a series of conversations, the general manager of the station offered me the job. I had spent the last twenty-four hours deliberating about the job description, expectations, and, most importantly, *the pay.*

I was married by then, and my husband is the perfect blend of wise advice and compassionate listening. He had been coaching me and helping me prepare for my meeting with the GM, presumably to accept the offer.

The problem was that the promotion didn't come with a pay raise. I was being promoted in title only. And, if you want to get to the real nitty-gritty, the hours were *worse.* The weekday morning anchor gets up around 3:00 a.m. to be on the desk for the morning show each day. It wasn't necessarily my dream job, but I was eager to get a full-time anchor position. It was the leg up I needed to advance my career.

I decided the early morning hours were something I could get used to, but what I couldn't swallow was the fact that I was being offered the promotion without a pay increase.

Sitting in the office with the general manager, I inquired why this was.

I must have drunk an extra cup of coffee with a spoonful of courage that morning, because I boldly asked, "Is this pay rate the same as the gentleman's I will be replacing?"

I did not get an answer to that question. Instead, the GM implied that the promotion and title should be enough for me. I should be grateful for the opportunity.

"This is a great move for you, April. This is an opportunity most of your colleagues are begging for."

Boom. There it was. The story line women have been fed all of our lives.

We should be grateful for the opportunities that come our way, for they could have just as easily been given to someone else. Or someone more agreeable!

We should be grateful someone is giving us the attention and fancy title.

We should be grateful for the job to begin with. Don't get ahead of yourself. Don't ask for more!

Just like when Sam had tried all those years earlier to help me be a "better" journalist, when I should have been grateful for his hurtful words and bullying ways.

I realized the pattern had been repeating itself. Sam used manipulation and aggression. The GM leaned on the culture of the male patriarchy in the news business. Either way, I felt oppressed.

I was disgusted and pissed. I knew I was ready and qualified for this job, and I wanted a pay raise.

I calmly looked up at the GM and slid the paperwork he was expecting me to sign back across the desk to him.

"I'm afraid I'll have to pass. If the job doesn't come with a raise, then I'll stay where I am in my current role."

I literally wanted to jump out of my chair and give myself a high five. I had delivered that line just as my husband and I had rehearsed it!

The general manager looked puzzled and shocked. "I'm really sorry to hear that, April. I felt certain we would walk out of here today with a deal."

"No deal, but thank you. I really appreciate it." (I had to add the thank-you and the appreciation, because I should be grateful, right?)

Within three months of that conversation, I made the decision to leave television news. It was a soul-sucking job, and the benefits and rewards simply weren't there. It was a rat race, and I didn't want to be a rat.

At this point in my life, something was stirring inside of me. A restlessness and a deep knowing that I had been made for more. Many people thought I was nuts for leaving such a high-profile and promising career . . . but deep down I was seeking something I couldn't find in the corporate setting: autonomy. I was curious what it would be like to create a path for myself that was fully my own.

The oppression bled throughout my young career like a bad rash I couldn't get rid of. I was agitated but didn't have a real vision yet how to cure it. Instinctively, I sensed that the only way to overcome the oppression was to be smarter than the oppressor.

I left my career behind to begin this new quest: to forge my own way, on my own terms, designing a future that would allow me to step more powerfully into a life I designed.

It was a huge shock to people when they learned I had left my job without a new job lined up! They assumed I was leaving because I had landed a better job in a larger market with a higher-profile position as anchor. It was hard for them to understand, but not once did I question my decision. It was one of the best decisions I ever made. It set me on a path to discovering who I am as a journalist and storyteller. Turns out, I am grateful to the GM. He presented me with a golden opportunity to discover what it feels like to exercise my voice. Sam had done that for me too, that day in the parking lot.

Both times I was nervous and shaky. My neck turned red, and my throat felt like it would close up completely, leaving me unable to breathe or swallow. However, a seed was planted in me. Those challenging situations were merely opportunities for me to exercise my voice, to claim my worth, and to stand firm in my power. My voice was in there somewhere, exercised in ways I didn't know I had in me, and the taste of it left me wanting more!

Believe me when I say it was *hard* to muster up the courage to face those two men and the many other Sams I've encountered in my career. They all came wearing different disguises, but their agenda was always the same: to exert power over me and to keep me quiet and in my place.

For more years than I care to admit, I dealt with this ongoing subtle abuse. It's sneaky. If you don't have your antennae on high alert, you'll miss it, and it will seep in without your permission.

I'd love to tell you that I got really good at defusing the Sams . . . but the truth is, I didn't. They kept showing up in my life because I hadn't quite figured out how to stop them. As they say, God will keep sending you the teacher until you learn the lesson.

It wasn't until many years later, when I made a big cross-country move, that I finally started listening to God and trusting myself at a whole new level. I often joke that I had to move back to Texas to find my Texas-sized big girl panties.

On a practical level, we moved to be closer to family.

My dad was in very poor health, and it was important to be closer to home to help with his needs.

On a spiritual level, I had to move to Texas to find my space.

Just a few years before our move, I had started writing and sharing my stories on social media. At first they were pretty neutral and innocent. They were full of encouragement and inspiration, but honestly, they were pretty vanilla and benign. I had also started a private community, and up until our move, the community had been pretty quiet. I created the space to invite women to share their stories, but I hadn't exactly figured out how to get them to show up and be bold with their voices.

I realize now it had to do with the fact that I was still trying to figure that out for myself!

Moving conjured up all sorts of feelings for me. It was a very emotional time, and the ground underneath me felt like quicksand. I had spent the previous eighteen years planting roots and investing in a home I loved, a community I loved, a city I loved, a church I loved, and friends I loved.

In Texas, I felt untethered.

Who were my people? Where was my community? What did I have to offer here? I felt like an outsider looking in. There was no sense of belonging for me.

So here I was—in a new home, in a new city, with no friends, no church, no coworkers (by now, I was running my own business and working from home), and no connection to tie me down and ground me. Yes, I had family here, but even that felt new to me, because we had spent nearly twenty years apart.

I turned to the only place I felt any sense of control and connection—the community I had built online called LIGHTbeamers. I deeply desired conversation and stimulation, so I began delivering prompts and storytelling challenges in an effort to get more members involved and showing up with their stories. I was starved for friendships and community, so I poured myself into this group. It was the only place I could find what I was looking for. I began to share my story, exposing vulnerable sides of myself that felt too big to hold inside anymore. Big cross-country moves are hard . . . and I was openly sharing my "hard" with them. This felt like therapy to me.

There were real, authentic moments, from sharing my heartbreak over moving to concerns around my dad's health. My emotions were just under the surface, and that surface was thin and fragile. I was on edge and riding the roller coaster day after day. One minute I was sad, the next minute I was angry. I covered most of it up with a smile and continued to throw myself into my work because it was the only thing that made me feel sane and in control.

Finally, about a year after our move, we began to look for a church. We had left behind an amazing church community, and it was important to find a place where our family could worship and meet new people. Our kids were also navigating their own emotions from the move, so we were looking for a youth group where they could dig in and connect with kids their age.

After hopping around for months to different churches, we finally settled on one that felt like a good fit for our family. We found ourselves getting connected, meeting new people, and really enjoying the Sunday sermons. The pastor seemed like a great guy, and he'd gone out of his way to make us feel welcomed as newcomers.

One Sunday after church, the pastor held an information session on the life of the church. All newcomers were invited to learn more about its mission and vision. The goal was to help us make an informed decision about whether we were ready to explore church membership.

My husband had a prior commitment, so I attended the meeting solo.

At first, it seemed everything the pastor was saying checked off all of our boxes.

- Theology
- Mission
- Giving
- Youth
- Community

But then he got to organizational development.

You see, this was a brand-new church, recently planted, without a lot of the constructs most churches have once they become established. There were no elders or deacons in place yet.

In Presbyterian churches, elders and deacons serve as leaders of the church, helping govern and make important decisions about the life of the congregation. I had served as a deacon at our previous church for three years. It was one of the most challenging and rewarding experiences of my life. Talk about service—church leadership is one where you literally have to remove yourself and think of others first. It was one of the most humbling experiences I'd ever been a part of, and I loved every minute of it!

The pastor explained that this new church was part of the Presbyterian Church in America (PCA). Our previous church was Presbyterian Church USA (PCUSA). I wasn't aware of the difference between the two denominations except that one was considered moderate and the other was a little more conservative.

Then, the pastor informed us that once this new church grew big enough to ordain elders and deacons, those roles would go only to the men.

INSERT HARD STOP.

Say what???

The leadership of this brand-new church, planted in the twenty-first century, will be handled only by the men?

Did I hear that correctly?

I asked a slew of probing questions, because surely I had misunderstood what he was saying.

Nope. This church and the doctrine of the PCA points toward men being the only ones God calls into office. This is not the case in the PCUSA; they have been ordaining women for decades.

Suddenly, I couldn't breathe. I could feel that old familiar feeling of my neck turning red and my throat closing up. I had to get out of there.

As soon as the meeting was adjourned, I said my polite goodbyes and thank-yous and made a quick escape. In the car, I burst into tears. Sobbing, I had to keep wiping my eyes so that I could see the road in front of me.

I was so distraught because I had just moved my family across the country into the land of back-ass thinking and belief systems. I had just given up the home I loved, the people I loved, the community I loved, and the church I loved—*for what?* All of the emotions I had been bottling up since this big move exploded like a firecracker. I was utterly overcome in that moment.

The very fact that my family had felt so at home at this church and felt called to become repeat visitors, and even give membership serious consideration, made me question *everything*.

Was I just nuts? Had I completely lost it?

Ever since stepping out on my own after leaving the news business all those years ago, I had forged my way in the world using my own skills and talents. And although I had encountered more Sams along the way, I hadn't hit roadblocks that denied me access simply because I was a woman. Sure, I'd felt slighted here and there, but nothing to this degree. In my mind, this took oppression to a whole new level.

This was all God's fault. I had heard His voice in the dead of night calling me home to Texas, and this is where He'd sent me?

"I don't know anyone here other than my sister," I cried out loud in the car, angry with God and His direction. "My dad's health is getting worse. I have no friends and no sense of community here . . . and the minute I start to feel comfy in this community of faith, you drop this hammer on me?"

There will be no women leaders of this church.
Because we women should be grateful, right? Grateful that God has ordained the men to be leaders, and left the easier roles up to us.

It's like all the Sams I'd ever encountered in my life were piled in the car with me like circus clowns with terrible merry-go-round music playing in the background, laughing at me and piercing me with their glee.

Take that, April.

All of my anger and frustration exploded to the top.

I called my husband on the way home. He couldn't make out a word I was saying as I heaved and sobbed and sputtered out things like, "I can't believe this" and "What the fuck?"

Thankfully, my husband has been there since the very first Sam experience, and he's watched my plight as a woman and become my most valued and treasured ally in the fight. Like he always does, he reassured me and did his best to calm me down. He reassured me that I wasn't crazy, and validated my feelings with his own statements like, "Of course women should be allowed into office. Anything less than that is antiquated and true lack-thinking."

Despite my husband's reassurances, I fell asleep that night doubting and questioning everything. I felt despondent, not just because of what I had learned at the church meeting, but because all the stories of women I had interviewed and worked with over the years flooded into my head and played on a continuous loop.

A few days later, the pastor emailed me inviting me to coffee. He's a smart guy. He'd noted my battery of questions at the information meeting and sensed my shock at what he'd shared. He invited me to an open conversation about my views and thoughts regarding women's roles in the church.

This isn't a story about the religious patriarchy—although I have a lot to say about it! What this is about is my decision to speak up and say something. The seed that had been planted all those years ago sprouted the night of the church meeting and in the days that followed as I examined the reality that women are still being "put in their place" in the most unlikely and sneaky spots. For years this was prevalent in my career, but now it had shown up in a place I value greatly—my church.

Remember when I said God keeps sending you the teachers until you learn the lesson?

God didn't send me to that church by accident. He sent me the mother of all Sams because He knew it would force me to get the message. And this one was my tipping point.

I'm not sure I would have had the same reaction had I not spent years climbing to the top of my career by navigating and breaking down countless established patriarchal systems and busting glass ceilings. Good journalists are trained to question and probe. As time went on, my voice got stronger the more I exercised it.

Also, I had experienced firsthand the opportunity to serve a church in a leadership role. And it wasn't just me—countless other women were doing important work ministering to people and helping churches make sound decisions.

Thinking about what had transpired with this new church, I realized I can't stay quiet. I can't keep running away when my neck gets red and my throat closes up.

I can't change a narcissist like Sam. I can't change the leadership of a television station. I can't change a church's specific doctrine. But what I can do is stand my ground and make my voice heard. I can be who I am fully—who God made me to be—and own my story and voice.

It's taken me a lot of soul-searching to really lean in and get this lesson.

The series of events that led to this awakening didn't happen by accident. Our stories are no accident.

I didn't "happen" to start a community like LIGHTbeamers and fill it with a bunch of women by accident.

I didn't move to Texas and get uprooted from everything for no good reason. Sometimes we need to be challenged to see things we otherwise would refuse to see. I was too comfortable in South Carolina. Everything I had created there was safe.

Moving back to Texas was a complete ungrounding for me. It made me reevaluate everything: my work, my circumstances, my community, my family, my relationships, my faith . . . and most importantly, my value.

What I realized is I can't run away and keep my voice to myself. I have to stand up for what I believe. I know in my heart of hearts God called me to withstand these tests so I could hone my skills to share the stories of the disenfranchised, the underserved, the overlooked, and the oppressed.

I could no longer not see what I saw, not feel what I felt.

And trust me, it's hard to speak up when, for generations, we've been told to keep quiet.

I accepted the pastor's invitation and joined him for coffee. I shared my story of being a deacon and how important it was to me to raise my kids in an environment where women are recognized and welcomed alongside men for their leadership abilities. He listened to me with grace. He didn't try to convince me that my beliefs were wrong. We simply came to the conclusion that we interpret scripture differently. He told me my views were welcome, and he encouraged me to have these conversations with more women in the church, admitting that I was not the only woman in the congregation who felt this way.

I left that meeting still a little shell-shocked yet also empowered.

In the months and years that have followed, I've come to realize the point of it all wasn't about women's equality (although it's a worthy and critical cause!) or my feminist agenda.

It was about discovering my true value, and in finding that, *I found my voice.*

Do I still attend that church? Actually, I do.

We've been attending regularly for over three years now, and trust me, I have days when I question what I'm doing there. Although the church and its people have many wonderful and redeeming qualities, I don't agree with their particular doctrine and stance on women leadership. I recently sat through the church's big announcement of its first elders being elected to office—both of them men. It's a big sticking point I've wrestled with nonstop. As someone who leads women and empowers them to share their stories and become better leaders in the world, I've felt like a fraud at times. I've had long, hard, difficult conversations with God over this one . . . and this is what I hear Him say every single time I have the urge to run away and find a new church:

"April, how do you expect to lead if you surround yourself only with people who think and believe exactly like you?"

I ran away from Sam. I left my job at the TV station. And in countless other situations, I looked for the easy way out.

We can't even begin to explore the depths of our voice if we speak it only into a vacuum chamber.

My job isn't to stay safe and comfortable anymore. My job is to call more women forward, and give them the tools and resources to discover their own value and voice. We must do this inside our organizations, our communities, our churches, and our families.

And so . . . I stay.

I stay because I trust God and I remain hopeful that I can be used appropriately as a light to others, especially for women!

Inside our LIGHTbeamers Community, we have women from all around the globe—from diverse cultures, opposing political views, vastly different backgrounds, and ways of thinking. Not once have I silenced these women from sharing their stories. I value what they have to say and give them a space to speak freely. I encourage them to test their own boundaries and comfort zones. I get them to question and probe their own beliefs and examine the boxes they may have allowed themselves to reside in a little too long.

I've created a place for them to be seen and heard. And in doing that work, I've encountered my own hard edges. My own small boxes have come into full view. I've had to find my voice in order to lead others to do the same.

It's funny to me now, thinking about women in leadership and where it has shown up for me in my life. Mostly it's been an inside job. I haven't had a lot of women leaders, especially not in my career. Most of those roles were held by men. Don't get me wrong—I've had some incredible male mentors and teachers along the way, like my two professors who heard me all those years ago when I was first testing the audible level of my voice. But I still want more. I want *more women* to stake their claim, own their story, and use their voice! There is just so much work to be done. We can't run away!

When we are comfortable, it's too easy to sit by and be "grateful" for what is ours.

When we step outside of our comfort zones, we are able to stretch and explore the depths of who we are, what we believe, and what we want to stand for. This is where we find our value and voice. No one else is going to do it for us—not even the women who are currently standing in the gap as leaders . . . because it's an inside job.

We need women leading inside our families, communities, jobs, and churches, and, most importantly, we need to lead ourselves.

The work is far from over. I'm a work in progress, too!

I don't regret any encounters or challenging conversations that have given me the opportunity to explore my voice. Some of them turned my stomach, and others made me angry and tossed me into despair. But each and every one of them gave me an opportunity to explore my deepest thoughts and my truest desires. They helped me define and claim my value and my power.

And for that, I *am* extremely grateful.

BE IN OUR NEXT BOOK

Have you dreamt of becoming a published author but felt stuck and overwhelmed about where to even begin? If you are shaking your head yes, then this is for you.

The She Gets Published: LIGHTbeamers Author Program is an opportunity to dip your toe into the world of writing and publishing without having to create an entire book or trying to figure things out in isolation.

Inside this 9-month group coaching program led by April Adams Pertuis (LIGHTbeamers) and Lanette Pottle (She Gets Published & Positivity Lady Press), you'll be guided every step of the way – from selecting and writing the right story, to creating your author platform, to marketing and selling your books.

You'll learn behind-the-scenes details of the publishing process as you work with a professional publisher and team of editors and book designers. PLUS the story you write inside the program will be published in the next release for the LIGHTbeamers collaborative book series - just like the women in this book.

Learn more and join the waitlist at www.lightbeamers.com/author

WORK WITH APRIL

April Adams Pertuis is a visibility and media specialist with a career spanning more than 30 years in the television and video industry. She is an award-winning journalist who has worked for CBS Television, HGTV, DIY Network, and the Food Network.

Today April works with people and brands to help them tell their story in a more authentic way so they can transform their lives and businesses.

April's passion is working with women - equipping and empowering them to share their stories in bigger, bolder ways. She has helped thousands of women step on stages, write books, create podcasts, build ministries, and exponentially grow their business and impact.

To learn more about working with April, book a free call: www.lightbeamers.com/apply

ABOUT LIGHTBEAMERS

April Adams Pertuis' passion for storytelling and creating community with women led her to create LIGHTbeamers - a safe space to explore your story, find support, and get training on how to excavate the layers of your story to use in a positive, powerful way.

Using the weekly story prompts and private community, members have open and honest conversations about life, business, personal growth, and spirituality. It's a place to learn more about storytelling as it relates to your own life and business.

LIGHTbeamers also offers online courses, group coaching, and training programs, as well as high-level mentorship for women leaders who are ready to step into their brave and share their story with more people.

Members are CEOs, entrepreneurs, spiritual and civic leaders, change-makers, missionaries, teachers, and healers.

They use their story every day to create community, affect change, and make a positive impact in the world by shining their light.

To learn more about the LIGHTbeamers community and suite of programs, go to www.lightbeamers.com

ABOUT THE INSIDE STORY PODCAST

The Inside Story Podcast takes you behind the curtain of the biggest success stories of entrepreneurs, thought leaders, and change-makers. . . people who have walked through fire and come out on the other side brighter. They aren't mechanical or scripted. They are unabashedly authentic and real. And they are generating massive success & fulfillment as a result!

The goal of the Inside Story is to inspire you to think about your own story, and learn to share it so it can shine a light for others.

Listen in to discover unique storytelling tips and mechanics that will empower you to tell your story in a whole new way. Learn more and listen at www.lightbeamers.com/podcast

ABOUT POSITIVITY LADY PRESS

Positivity Lady Press is a small indie publishing imprint dedicated to awakening possibilities in the lives of women through inspirational, self help and personal development books. The press is owned and operated by Lanette Pottle.

WE BELIEVE when we encourage, empower, and elevate women, the world becomes a kinder, more compassionate place.

WE BELIEVE when women rise to their full potential it generates an endless supply of creative solutions to the challenges facing our world.

WE BELIEVE thoughtful collaboration among women accelerates the speed and the reach of positive impact we can make.

WE BELIEVE women's voices matter and a book is a powerful way to amplify them.

If you have ideas for collaborative projects elevating the voices of women, connect with Lanette directly through email at lanette@lanettepottle.com

ABOUT OUR PAY-IT-FORWARD PARTNERSHIP

 100% of royalties from Amazon sales of this book will be directed to KIVA, with a special interest given to funding micro-loans to help women start and grow businesses.

Kiva is an international nonprofit, founded in 2005 in San Francisco, with a mission to expand financial access to help underserved communities thrive.

They do this by crowdfunding loans and unlocking capital for the underserved, improving the quality and cost of financial services, and addressing the underlying barriers to financial access around the world. Through Kiva's work, students can pay for tuition, women can start businesses, farmers are able to invest in equipment and families can afford needed emergency care.

Learn more at www.kiva.org

Made in United States
North Haven, CT
29 October 2022

26075786R00157